AMAZING

ST. LOUIS

To Norma Jean /
Keep that dial on
KMOX and KETC 9!

P.S... and KETC 9!

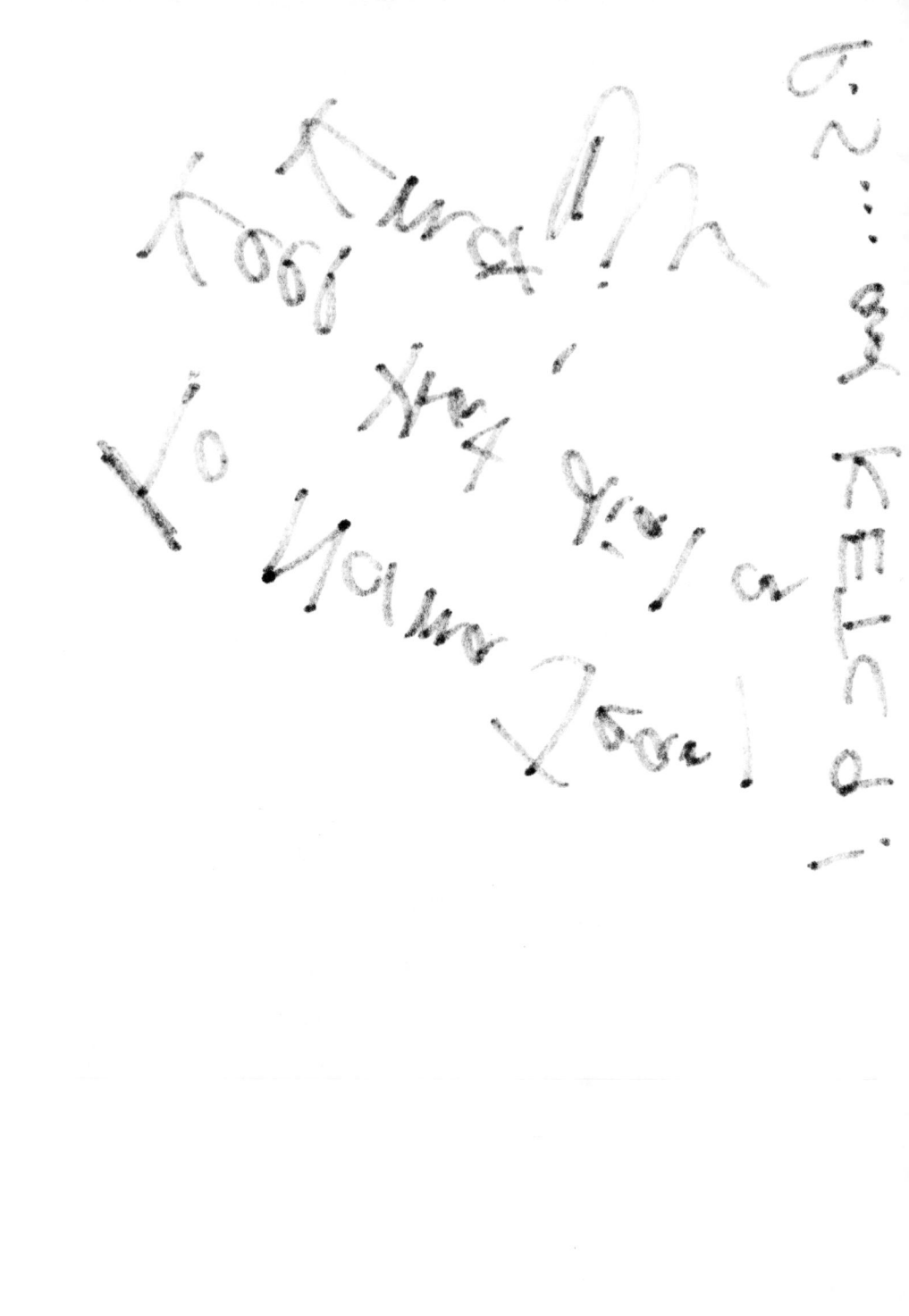

250 Years
of Great Tales
and Curiosities

AMAZING
ST. LOUIS

FEATURING

STORIES ABOUT **MARK TWAIN**, THE **EXORCIST**,
DARTH VADER, THE **CIA**, AND **JACK** THE **RIPPER**

CHARLIE BRENNAN

REEDY PRESS
St. Louis, Missouri

For Beth

Reedy Press
PO Box 5131
St. Louis, MO 63139
www.reedypress.com

Library of Congress Control Number: 2013950325

ISBN: 978-1-935806-56-1

Design by Jill Halpin

Printed in the United States of America
14 15 16 17   5 4 3 2

Contents

Section 2   St. Louisans Who Changed the World

Section 3   They Didn't Teach Me That in School

Section 4 Strange St. Louis Pairings

Section 5 They Overcame Hardship

Section 6 I Didn't Know There Was a St. Louis Connection

Section 7 Dark St. Louis

Section 8   The Ten Amazing and Often Overlooked St. Louis Sports Stories

Acknowledgments

Thanks to the guys at Reedy Press, Matthew Heidenry and Josh Stevens. Matt turned some really rough writing into a beautiful book reflecting the class and style of St. Louis. Josh was encouraging from the start; if it has anything to do with St. Louis, Josh supports it. Both Stevens and Heidenry are such treasures in literary St. Louis. I'm proud to be part of the Reedy Press family!

For the past twenty-five years, I learned a lot about St. Louis from the fascinating people I interviewed. For this project, I am especially grateful to Bill Iseminger, William Webster, Tim Weiner, the late Stephen E. Ambrose, the late James Neal Primm, Carol Ferring Shepley, Scott Berg, John H. Exton, H. W. Brands, Michael Beschloss, Thomas Maier, Kevin Phillips, the late William Barnaby Faherty, S.J., David Fiedler, Dan Viets, the late Ken Kaufman, Harper Barnes, Daniel Shea, David Herbert Donald, Robert Ellis, Yogi Berra, Greg Marecek, Rex Sinquefield, John Taylor, Larry Merritt, Wally Moon, Bruce Jenkins, Taylor Hackford, Dan Barks, the late Earl Weaver, the late Barry Commoner, A. E. Hotchner, Burt Bacharach, Marsha Mason, Dave Simons, Sue Lordi, James Earl Jones, John Schneiter, Gregg Allman, Lou Gramm, Russell Errett, Buzz Bissinger, Adrienne Barbeau, Linda Blair, the late Jack Buck, Jo Jo White, Bob Pettit, Bill White, and Denny McLain.

CBS Executive Producer Peggy Cohill arranged many of these interviews. She is the best in the business, shares my interest for our region, and—to be sure—I am so fortunate to have worked with her for a quarter of a century.

Gotta give props to my closest colleagues at the Mighty 'MOX who provide a stimulating daily environment: Chris Mihill, Debbie Monterrey, and Steve Moore. They keep me on my toes and smiling. And to my office mates Doug McElvein and Mark Reardon, true pros who put up with my ramblings and messy desk.

Huge thanks to my great kids, Charlie and Lynly. When I was working on the book, I was not spending time with them. I owe you guys. And I must express my deepest heartfelt gratitude to my wonderful wife, Beth, who for some reason supports all my crazy endeavors, like this one.

Introduction

My job is to talk about St. Louis. And every weekday for the past twenty-five years, I have heard one story after another about this area. Once in a while, a tale makes me sit up in my chair and say, "Wow! I gotta put that one in the file!"

When the cabinet got full, I pulled out all the files, selected the best of the best stories, shortened them, and created what I think are "greatest hits" of St. Louis people and history.

My opinion? St. Louis is an amazing place with an amazing history. How can you read these chapters and come to any other conclusion?

After all, a St. Louisan became the first American woman to win a Nobel Prize in medicine. The first city in North America was . . . here. We invented the cocktail party and the first desktop computer.

Because of someone from these parts, the world got Chicago, Twitter, peanut butter, index funds, and a conviction for Al Capone.

It's safe to say most of us don't think St. Louisans saved the nation, invented rock and roll, sparked the Civil War, started the Mexican Revolution, ended the Cold War, and saved French wine. But, in story after story, as we'll see in succeeding pages, that's how it's seen outside of St. Louis.

St. Louis also has its share of odd and strange stories to offset its great contributions to culture and society. For everyone's entertainment and edification, I threw those in also.

I hope readers learn something new about St. Louis and conclude that it really is amazing. Maybe a few will commit the stories to memory, tell them with pride and start bragging about our area. And, hopefully, the newfound sense of civic spirit will inspire others to greatness (to be included in the next edition, of course).

Section One

St. Louis Firsts and Foremosts

America's First City

Your teachers taught you the first cities in the United States were St. Augustine, Jamestown, or Plymouth. Oh, they meant well—but they were wrong.

St. Louis is home to the first city in America. I kid you not. Between 900 AD and the mid-1300s AD, 10,000 to 20,000 Indians known as Mississippians lived in a six-square-mile area in what is now Collinsville, Illinois. This city was larger than London at the time.

Farmers, fishermen, and hunters populated the city. A paramount chief oversaw the construction of earthen mounds, a defensive wall, a stockade, a large ceremonial plaza, and a sun calendar known as a woodhenge. The Mississippians built about 120 mounds, of which 70 still exist. Historians speculate that they used the mounds for religious purposes, rituals, government buildings, homes, or graves.

Today, the location is a United Nations Educational, Scientific, and Cultural Organization (UNESCO) site known as Cahokia Mounds.

Cahokia, however, is a misnomer. The site, as stated earlier, is actually in Collinsville, not in nearby Cahokia, Illinois. To add to the confusion, Cahokian Indians moved to the area in the 1600s, 300 years after this city—and the Mississippians—vanished.

Another misnomer: The 100-foot-tall Monks Mound is named after French monks who did not build this or any mound. From 1809 until 1813, they lived on a nearby smaller mound. If ever there were people who got undeserved naming rights, they would be these monks! After all, by getting their

"Cahokia" Mound, 1907. Courtesy Library of Congress

name on the centerpiece mound made of 22 million cubic feet of soil, these monks were memorialized on the largest prehistoric earthen monument in all the Americas! Indeed, the *New York Times* called Monks Mound, "North America's first imposing piece of architecture."

Amazingly, in addition to building mounds, the Mississippians traded as far north as Canada, as far south as the Gulf of Mexico, and as far east as the South Appalachians. That's a lot of territory for people who had no horses, cars, or even wheels.

The Mississippian city utterly vanished about 100 years

before Columbus reached America. Nobody knows why. Perhaps the area's resources declined. Warfare, climate change, and drought are the suspected reasons.

What did they call themselves? What language did they speak? No one knows.

Do descendants of the Mississippians live among us? No studies have been conducted to link the DNA of these Mississippians to modern persons.

Despite being the first and largest city ever built north of Mexico for hundreds of years, Cahokia Mounds does not get the attention of the ruins of the Aztecs, Incas, or the Mayans.

As the *Washington Post* stated,
Cahokia is
one of the best-kept
archaeological secrets in the country.

How different are we from the ancient Mississippians?

The Mississippians admired a "bird man" who symbolized the upper world. Similarly, today's St. Louisans admire men who wear cardinals on their uniforms.

The First Mobile Phone

Here's one you can ask your beer buddies: The first flight was in Kitty Hawk. The first commandment came from Mt. Sinai. Where do you think the mobile phone originated?

How about St. Louis on June 17, 1946.

Southwestern Bell was the first provider of the phone, developed by Bell Labs and AT&T with equipment from Motorola. Officially known as Mobile Telephone Service (MTS), these phones operated from trucks or cars. Monsanto and a contractor, Henry Perkinson, were the first subscribers, according to *American Heritage of Invention and Technology* magazine.

The "phone" had six radio channels and was constantly issuing busy signals. Although bulky and expensive, the phones were popular and distributed to twenty-five markets following their St. Louis launch. By 1948, mobile telephones were used by 5,000 customers in 100 cities and highway corridors.

Users first had to search their phones' six radio channels for a vacant frequency. If one was not in use, the caller pushed a "talk" button on the phone and gave the operator the phone number of the intended party. The operator connected calls through a switchboard. Only one party could talk at a time.

A monthly subscription cost $15 and a three-minute call cost 35 cents—$174 and $4.06, respectively, in 2012 dollars. The phone and its transmitter, located in the trunk, weighed about eighty pounds.

Tell your friends you are from St. Louis—home of the mobile phone!

The First Gas Station

St. Louis may not be home to the first automobile, but it was home to the first gas station. Operated by the Automobile Gasoline Company in 1905 and located at 412 S. Theresa Avenue, the station featured a garden hose, which, thanks to gravity, delivered gasoline from a large aboveground storage tank to a car. The facility did not offer food, car repair, restrooms, or even window squeegees.

Prior to the Automobile Gasoline Company's filling station, motorists went to a druggist, bicycle shop, livery stable, or general store to buy gasoline in containers. Filling a car with gasoline sometimes required two or more people. One person held a funnel covered with a chamois cloth to filter impurities from the gasoline.

St. Louisans Harry Grenner and Clem Laessig, founders of the Automobile Gasoline Company, streamlined the process by using hoses with filters. They also pioneered the first use of gauges to measure gasoline. Grenner and Laessig eventually owned about forty gas stations.

15¢

Approximately 250 cars existed in St. Louis in 1905, and their drivers paid approximately 15 cents per gallon.

Braille: Children's Classroom Mischief Led to a National Trend

Dr. Simon Pollak, a board member at the Missouri School for the Blind in the late 1850s, visited France because he heard students there were teaching each other a new form of communication called Braille. Pollak returned to St. Louis and recommended Braille's adoption at his school.

His idea encountered criticism because some thought blind individuals writing Braille would be separated from those unable to read it. And, absurdly, one administrator felt Braille "was not pleasing to the eye" (I know, I know).

But the students of the school, located then on Chestnut Street between Sixth and Seventh streets, began to communicate with each other using Braille, finding it relatively easy to read and write. They also liked passing messages—"even love letters"—their teachers could not decipher. The fun did not last long for the school's teachers adopted Braille and began teaching it in 1860.

At that moment, the Missouri School for the Blind in St. Louis became the first in the nation to read and write using the Braille method.

The First Index Fund

Index funds—mutual funds comprised of stocks tracking the components of a particular market—are very popular among investors. Something like this had to be the creation of a Wall Street genius, right?

Genius? Probably. Wall Street? No. The index fund was invented by a financier who spent much of his childhood in a St. Louis orphanage.

Seven-year-old Rex Sinquefield entered the St. Vincent Orphan Home in the early 1950s after his father died and his mother experienced difficulty caring for him. With 120 other orphans, Sinquefield studied with nuns, completed chores, and listened to Cardinals baseball on the radio. And, according to *St. Louis Magazine*, he "choked back the tears of homesickness."

"My younger brother Jerry was with me," Sinquefield says. "Looking back, the experience was clearly beneficial. Of course, most kids at the time wanted to be back home with their families, and most kids didn't realize their families were not in positions to take care of them."

Sinquefield describes St. Vincent's as a "run-of-the-mill nineteenth-century orphanage, although I was there in the twentieth century. It was the kind of institution you would see in *Oliver Twist* with large dormitory rooms. But we were safe and well cared for. And we were loved by thirty German nuns. It was a very, very healthy environment and certainly much better than any of us would have had at the time."

Other than the electrical and mechanical work, Rex and the other boys maintained the facility. They swept, mopped, scrubbed, and waxed floors covering about 300,000 square feet of space in the St. Vincent's Home at 7401 Florissant Road. "We kept that place spotless," he recalls.

Sinquefield remained there until he attended Bishop DuBourg High School. After high school, Rex was off to the seminary. While studying for the priesthood, Sinquefield also studied the stock market and owned $200 worth of Great Northern paper stock.

He left the seminary for Saint Louis University and the University of Chicago's School of Business. In college, he learned about the efficiency of markets. After completing his studies, Sinquefield worked at the American National Bank of Chicago.

On September 4, 1973, he created the first S&P 500 Index Fund in the galaxy!

The new fund was a mutual fund consisting of all the stocks listed on the S&P 500. Two years later in 1975, the Vanguard 500 Index Fund was started by John Bogle.

By 1981, Sinquefield was co-founder of Dimensional Fund Advisors (DFA), which sold, you guessed it, index funds. After making untold millions at DFA, Sinquefield retired in 2005.

The First Director of Central Intelligence

On January 24, 1946, Rear Admiral Sidney W. Souers, a St. Louis insurance executive, became the first director of Central Intelligence. President Harry Truman, at a White House lunch, gave Souers a black hat, a black cloak, and a wooden dagger. Apparently alcohol was served because Truman then knighted Souers chief of the "Cloak and Dagger Group of Snoopers" and "Director of Centralized Snooping."

Despite the president's playful antics, Souers was suddenly in charge of an organization called the Central Intelligence Group with 2,000 staffers and files on more than 400,000 individuals.

Souers had not sought the job. When asked about his plans, he exclaimed, "I want to go home." After about 100 days, he quit the job. According to historian Tim Weiner, Souers left behind a single important top-secret memo:

> **There is an urgent need to develop the highest possible quality of intelligence on the USSR in the shortest possible time.**

About a year later, on September 18, 1947, the Central Intelligence Group became the Central Intelligence Agency.

Cloak -and- Dagger

Souers remained an unofficial advisor to President Truman. In 1950, he warned the president that anti-communist hysteria was as dangerous as communism itself.

Admiral Souers returned to St. Louis in 1953. He became chairman of General American Life Insurance Company in 1954 and served as the company's president from 1957 to 1958. He also served as a director or trustee of the Bi-State Development Agency, St. Luke's Hospital, and Lindenwood College.

In his final years, Souers lived at 625 Skinker Boulevard. After a long illness, Souers died on January 14, 1973, at the age of eighty at St. Luke's Hospital.

The First Cocktail Party

Others live proudly in cities that pioneered penicillin (London), democracy (Athens), or religion (Jerusalem). In that spirit, St. Louisans should stand tall knowing one of their own brought forth a development that has certainly made this planet a better place to live: the cocktail party.

In May of 1917, Mrs. Julius Walsh threw a party at her Central West End mansion that is considered the world's first cocktail party. The *St. Paul Pioneer Press* reported, "Positively the newest stunt in society is the giving of 'cocktail parties.'" Apparently, before Mrs. Walsh, nobody had attended "cocktail parties," for she was credited with being "responsible for the innovation."

Fifty people attended the party, which took place at noon on a Sunday. A meal was served at 1 p.m. According to the *Wall Street Journal*, drinks included "Bronx cocktails (gin, dry vermouth, sweet vermouth and orange juice) . . . Clover Leafs (gin, grenadine, lime juice and egg white, garnished with a mint leaf) . . . Highballs—'some with Scotch and some with rye or Bourbon whisky'—along with Gin Fizzes and at least one Mint Julep 'for a former gentleman of Virginia' . . . a potent Sazerac (whiskey, sugar and Peychaud's bitters in an absinthe-rinsed glass). And yes, there were Martinis and Manhattans."

"The party was an instant hit," according to the *St. Paul Pioneer Press*. The story was picked up by newspapers around the country and Mrs. Walsh's innovation spread nationwide.

The Walsh mansion at 4510 Lindell Boulevard is today home to the archbishop of the Catholic Archdiocese of St. Louis!

The First Float Trip?

Before Lewis and Clark embarked on their historic journey to the Pacific Northwest, they had to shop for provisions in St. Louis. This list was sundry: flour, mosquito nets, salt port, ground corn, shirts, flags, etc.

And records show, on April 9, 1804, Meriwether Lewis bought 100 gallons of whiskey at $1.28 each and 20 gallons of whiskey at $1 each.

That's why the Corps of Discovery has been described as a "party" of thirty-three.

A Football First

St. Louisans are well aware their city gave toasted ravioli, gooey butter cake, and Budweiser to the world, but few know their city offered up an even more important contribution: football's forward pass. (Well, maybe not as important as Budweiser.)

In the early part of the twentieth century, several national newsmagazines ran stories exposing the violence and brutality of college football. Many colleges sought to ban the sport. President Teddy Roosevelt, afraid of losing this "manly" activity, encouraged colleges to revise their rules instead.

In 1905, John Heisman, Georgia Tech's coach, encouraged the Intercollegiate Rules Committee to approve the forward pass. Heisman had seen the pass used—illegally—when he coached at Auburn. Heisman felt the forward pass would "scatter the mob" and open up the game. According to Heisman, "With the forward pass, speed would supplant bull strength. Lighter, faster men would succeed beefy giants whose

Courtesy Saint Louis University Libraries Special Collections

crushing weight maimed or killed their opponents."

The rules were changed to allow the forward pass in 1906. At the time, the penalties for incompletions were stiff, so the new play did not become popular quickly.

Saint Louis University coach Eddie Cochems had been an early advocate of the forward pass and was ready to implement it once the rules changed. "I took the team (St. Louis) to Lake Beulah, north of Chicago, in July, 1906, for the sole purpose of studying and developing the pass," Cochems recalled.

In a game against Carroll College on September 5, 1906, quarterback Bradley Robinson threw an incomplete pass on his first attempt. On his second try, Robinson threw twenty yards to Jack Schneider.

At that moment, Saint Louis University became the first school to officially— and successfully—complete a forward pass!

Saint Louis University went on to win the game, 22-0, and an undefeated 11-0 season.

In a cruel twist of irony, the school that started football's forward pass no longer has a football team.

The First Reports of the *Titanic* Were Written on Toilet Paper

Carlos Hurd of the *St. Louis Post-Dispatch* was the first reporter to interview the survivors of the unsinkable *RMS Titanic* after the mighty ship sank on April 15, 1912.

Indeed, this was an odd accomplishment for a reporter from St. Louis, a city nowhere near the North Atlantic. As it turned out, Hurd and his wife, Katherine, were on vacation on the *Carpathia*, which left New York on April 11 for Naples, Italy.

The *Carpathia* was the only ship to respond to the *Titanic*'s SOS. It rescued *Titanic* passengers and crew members from lifeboats. Returning to New York over the next three days, Carlos and Katherine interviewed the survivors.

Group of rescued on Carpathia

Survivors aboard *Carpathia*, of which Hurd was a passenger.
Courtesy Library of Congress

Hurd scored the first interviews because management of the *Carpathia* refused to deliver stateside reporters' telegrams to passengers. And, of course, news organizations in New York could not reach the ship by telephone or helicopter.

But Hurd was also hindered because the *Carpathia* crew was instructed to keep him away from survivors. Nor was he allowed to use the ship's telegraph to convey his story or receive wires from the *Post-Dispatch* or its affiliated newspapers.

Hurd faced another problem: a limited amount of paper. *Carpathia* Captain Arthur Rostron ordered all stationery removed from the ship's writing salons. Using whatever scraps of paper he could find, Hurd pieced together a 5,000-word story. When he ran out of parchment, he used toilet paper. Afraid their story would be confiscated, Katherine sat on their notes and completed pages.

Carlos Hurd suspected his bosses would greet the *Carpathia* with a vessel in New York. He wrapped his story in a cigar box and, lest the package fall into the water, threw in some champagne corks for buoyancy.

When the *Carpathia* reached the New York harbor, a tugboat hired by the *New York Evening World*, a Pulitzer publication like the *Post-Dispatch*, pulled up alongside. Hurd threw the box to Charles Chapin, city editor of the *Evening World*, whom he had met during an informal visit before he left New York.

The exclusive *Titanic* story from the view of its surviving passengers appeared that day in the *New York Evening World* and a day later in the *St. Louis Post-Dispatch*.

One of the greatest stories in journalism was written, in part, on toilet paper. And the scoop belonged to a St. Louisan.

The First Public School System to Offer Kindergarten

Maybe the most enduring trend to originate in St. Louis involved five- and six-year-old children.

St. Louis was the first school district in the United States to offer kindergarten thanks to the determination of Susan Blow, a St. Louisan whose father made a fortune in the lead industry and was later the U.S. minister to Brazil.

Carondelet Historic Center
St. Louis, Missouri
1873

In 1871, Blow toured Europe and examined classroom exercises for children ages three to six. Many of the lesson plans she observed were the creation of Friedrich Froebel, a pioneer in early childhood education. In 1872, Blow studied with Maria Bolte, a Froebel protégé who had opened a private kindergarten in New York with the idea of helping kids transition from family to school. In kindergarten, children learned shapes, colors, numbers, silence, hygiene, and drawing. Together, Blow and Bolte "worked to develop a program for public schools that would influence education forever."

Blow's first kindergarten was set up in the Des Peres School in Carondelet in 1872. She had three assistants helping the almost seventy students whose curriculum was centered on play and creativity.

By 1878, the board overseeing the St. Louis schools adopted kindergarten citywide. By 1881, both black and white children in St. Louis became the first in the nation to enjoy access to kindergarten instruction.

Blow accepted no pay for her work.

Soon, Blow and educators from St. Louis fanned the country teaching kindergarten methods to educators in Boston, Baltimore, Chicago, and a dozen other cities. Less than twenty-five years later, almost 200,000 children nationwide were enrolled in public kindergarten thanks to the advocacy of Blow and her fellow St. Louis educators. Blow had "led the entire nation in establishing standards for schools in kindergarten education."

By the time Blow died in 1916, more than 400 cities in the United States followed the St. Louis example and offered kindergarten.

The First Desktop Computer

The saga of William S. Burroughs is bittersweet, for the twenty-six-year-old New Yorker moved to St. Louis in 1881 full of ambition. He worked hard to succeed, and succeed he did. But Burroughs was ultimately unable to enjoy his success.

After years of trial and error, Burroughs invented the world's first adding machine in St. Louis in 1891. With the financial backing of St. Louis investors, his American Arithmometer Company sold the machines—which could add numbers and print the results—for the equivalent of $12,000 today.

> As historian Carol Ferring Shepley points out, Burroughs created the first computer to sit on a desktop.

Sadly, Burroughs died of tuberculosis in 1898, just six years after inventing the adding machine. In 1904, the newly named Burroughs Adding Machine Company moved to Detroit when Michigan officials offered the company ten free acres of land. Within two decades, sales reached into the millions.

The Other William S. Burroughs

What if William S. Burroughs had lived to meet his grandson and namesake William S. Burroughs, born in 1914?

Ironically, the business-like Burroughs family produced a second William Burroughs, an anti-establishment, drug-addicted scion later considered one of the most disruptive forces in American literature.

An associate of Beat writers Jack Kerouac and Allen Ginsberg, the younger Burroughs combined satire with the irrational and the surreal. His most famous book was *Naked Lunch*, published in 1953. Burroughs coined various terms, including "heavy metal" and "steely dan." The rock group Duran Duran's song "Wild Boys" is named after Burroughs's 1971 novel of the same name.

Burroughs's tragic life included the death of his second wife, which occurred when, like William Tell, he tried to shoot a glass of water off her head in Mexico City. He missed, escaped a murder conviction, and spent no significant time in jail.

Burroughs died at age eighty-three in 1997 in Kansas. He is buried in St. Louis's Bellefontaine Cemetery next to his grandfather.

Again, what if his grandfather had lived beyond forty-three years old? Would he have inspired his grandson to another direction—perhaps the business world? What would Donald Fagan and Walter Becker have named their band?

The First German-American U.S. Senator

Carl Schurz was born near Cologne, Germany, in 1829. In 1848, Schurz joined the revolution in Germany and, when almost captured, escaped through a sewer to France. Schurz turned around, returned to Germany in disguise, and then bribed a prison guard to lower his political mentor down the side of the prison's outer walls so Schurz could transport him to freedom in Scotland.

Schurz then emigrated to the United States. He got involved in politics in Wisconsin, was appointed minister to Spain, and, after serving as a major general in the Union Army during the Civil War, moved to St. Louis in 1867 to edit the *Westliche Post* newspaper, which he also co-owned.

Carl Schurz. Courtesy Library of Congress

Carl Schurz won a U.S. Senate seat from Missouri in 1869, becoming, at age forty, the first German-American U.S. senator.

Schurz served Missouri in the Senate until 1875. He became Secretary of the Interior, an editor of the *New York Evening Post*, and a columnist for *Harper's Weekly*.

I am getting tired just *typing* his accomplishments.

Schurz and other German-American editors are memorialized today in "The Naked Truth," a monument by sculptor Wilhelm Wandschneider. The memorial generated controversy when commissioned in 1913 for it portrayed a woman's full frontal nudity. The display was approved, then revoked, and then, when given the blessing of its primary benefactor, brewer Adolphus Busch, approved again.

During World War I, the Women's Christian Temperance Union suggested the bronze statue be melted down and "utilized for munition purposes." Instead, it survived both world wars.

Today it can be seen in the Compton Hill Reservoir Park.

Gracie Mansion, the official residence for the mayor of New York, is located in Carl Schurz Park in the Upper East Side of Manhattan.

The First African-American U.S. Senator

After he lived and worked in St. Louis, Hiram Rhodes Revels became the first African-American to serve in the U.S. Congress.

Revels was born a free man in Fayetteville, North Carolina, in 1827. Although Missouri forbade free blacks to live in the state for fear they would instigate uprisings, Revels moved to St. Louis anyway in 1852 because he understood "the law was seldom enforced." In St. Louis, Revels served as a pastor of the African Methodist Church at the corner of Seventh and Washington streets in St. Louis in 1853.

He later remembered, "I sedulously refrained from doing anything that would incite slaves to run away from their masters. It being understood that my object was to preach the gospel to them, and improve their moral and spiritual condition, even slave holders were tolerant of me."

Hiram Revels. Courtesy Library of Congress

Nonetheless, Revels was "imprisoned in Missouri in 1854 for preaching the gospel to Negroes." Revels operated a secret school in 1856 to teach African-Americans to read and write. He had about 150 pupils. The move was risky, because educating blacks was outlawed in 1847. According to historian William E. Parrish, it was "the earliest known Negro-run school in St. Louis."

Revels left St. Louis and attended Knox College in Galesburg, Illinois, graduating in 1857. He was one of the few college-educated black men in the United States. He later moved to Baltimore and then returned to St. Louis in 1863 to establish a school for emancipated slaves. He helped form a "Negro board of education."

Revels later moved to Mississippi, where the state legislature on January 20, 1870, voted him to represent the state as a U.S. senator.

At that moment,
Hiram Rhodes Revels,
the former St. Louis
preacher and educator,
became the first African-American
to serve in Congress!

The First Tweet

On March 21, 2006, Jack Dorsey, a native of St. Louis who attended Bishop DuBourg High School, sent out the world's first tweet on Twitter, the social media website he created.

In St. Louis, he co-founded Twitter, a social media platform allowing users to communicate quickly and easily by sending "tweets" of 140 characters or fewer. Dorsey has served as chairman and CEO of Twitter. The company claims 200 million active monthly users, who generate 400 million tweets every day.

Dorsey's first tweet from his account @Jack: "Just setting up my twttr."

Dorsey's invention is universal. Twitter was credited with allowing people to spread information and keep in touch with relatives during Japan's 2011 earthquake and tsunami. Twitter was also used by opposition groups in the Arab Spring. "By inventing Twitter, Jack may have well brought down dictators in

President Clinton's First Tweet

Bill Clinton sent his very first tweet in St. Louis on April 6, 2013. During an interview with Comedy Central's Stephen Colbert during the Clinton Global Initiative held at Washington University, the forty-second president sent the following, "Just spent amazing time with Colbert! Is he sane? He is cool! #cgiu!"

Colbert took the liberty of setting up the account for the former president using the twitter name @PrezBillyJeff. Mr. Clinton changed his handle a few weeks later to @billclinton.

The First Lady's First Tweet

First Lady Michelle Obama's first tweet took place in St. Louis before Game 1 of the World Series on October 19, 2011. Using a laptop in a room at Busch Stadium, Mrs. Obama asked her aides, "And now I just press 'tweet?'" Then she tweeted: "Military families serve our nation too. Let's all show our appreciation by @JoiningForces with them. Get involved: JoiningForces.gov. —mo" Among her first followers: Tom Hanks, Oprah Winfrey, and Steven Spielberg. That evening, the St. Louis Cardinals beat the Texas Rangers 3–2.

North Africa and the Middle East. That's not bad going for one guy," claims Twitter investor Richard Branson.

"What's most meaningful is the content that people are pushing out," Dorsey says. "Whether you have 45 million followers like Justin Bieber of just sixty, you can have a tweet that goes around the world. It's an international conversation."

McDonnell Built First Plane Designed to Land on Carriers

The first jet designed to take off and land on an aircraft carrier was developed in St. Louis by McDonnell Aircraft.

On July 21, 1946, the FH-1 Phantom, built at the Lambert–St. Louis plant, landed on a United States aircraft carrier. About sixty FH-1s were built. The British first landed a plane on a moving ship in 1917 but the St. Louis–built FH-1 was the first specifically *designed* for the purpose.

James S. McDonnell, founder and board chairman of the company, liked to name his machines after spirits: phantom, banshee, voodoo, goblin, demon. He believed inanimate objects had, in a sense, a life of their own, and he valued the workplace "spirit" needed to build magnificent machines.

In St. Louis McDonnell Aircraft also produced the F-101 Voodoo, which set the world speed record at 1,207.6 miles per hour on December 12, 1957. The company also built the F-4 Phantom II in St. Louis starting in the late 1950s. "The F-4 established 16 speed, altitude and time-to-climb records. In 1959, its prototype set the world altitude record at 98,556 feet. In 1961, an F-4 set the world speed record at 1,604 mph on a 15-mile circuit."

Again, all of these planes were built in St. Louis.

FH-1 Phantom in flight, 1948.
Courtesy U.S. Navy National Museum of Naval Aviation

Reaching the Stars with Mercury and Gemini

In the 1950s and 1960s, St. Louis was out of this world. St. Louis–based McDonnell Aircraft produced the first spacecraft taking Americans into space.

On May 5, 1961, Alan Shepard Jr. became the first NASA astronaut launched into outer space. He piloted the *Freedom 7* spacecraft, a Mercury capsule made in St. Louis. Astronaut John Glenn also traveled on a product made in St. Louis when, on February 20, 1962, he became the first American to orbit Earth by flying aboard *Friendship 7*.

In addition to the Mercury craft, McDonnell Aircraft manufactured the vehicles in the subsequent Gemini program. While the Mercury program launched Americans into space, the Gemini program (named because the craft had two seats, as in twins. Get it?) helped Americans perfect the technique of rendezvous and joining of space vehicles, a necessary preliminary to landing people on the moon.

McDonnell founder James S. McDonnell disliked use of the word "capsule" (sounded too much like a pill) and preferred to use "spacecraft." He also pronounced the word "Gemini" with a long *i* at the end (jem-uh-neye) because he felt the popular alternative (jem-uh-nee) sounded too much like a cricket.

The First Skyscraper

Is St. Louis home to the first skyscraper? Indeed, some say the first building to emphasize height and express verticality is the Wainwright Building at Seventh and Chestnut streets in downtown St. Louis. Designed by Chicago architect Louis Sullivan in 1889 for brewer Ellis Wainwright, the building remains one of the most famous and influential buildings in the world.

Calling the Wainwright one of the ten buildings that changed America, authors Dan Protess and Geoffrey Baer remind us, "It might seem obvious that skyscrapers should look tall. But they never did until this St. Louis tower reached toward the heavens in 1891."

In fact, according to Paul Goldberger, architecture critic for *Vanity Fair*, prior to Sullivan's Wainwright Building in St. Louis, "A lot of tall buildings looked like short buildings just made bigger. Or, in some cases even, two or three short buildings piled on top of each other."

In his design for the Wainwright Building, Sullivan recessed the horizontal spandrels over and underneath the windows. Meanwhile, he pushed forward or projected the vertical pilasters, which run uninterrupted up and down the building. Thus, because the Wainwright Building's horizontal lines are pushed back and its vertical lines are pushed forward, the building emphasizes height, a remarkable departure from buildings at the time.

Sullivan's colleague Frank Lloyd Wright wrote, "This was a great St. Louis moment. Here was the 'skyscraper:' a new thing beneath the sun . . . with virtue, individuality, beauty all its own."

America's Tallest Man-made Monument

Where is the nation's tallest man-made national monument? Here's a clue: this book is about St. Louis superlatives. If you did NOT guess St. Louis, please read the front cover of this book again. Everyone else can proceed.

- The Gateway Arch is the highest national monument at 630 feet.
- The Space Needle in Seattle is 603 feet.
- The San Jacinto Monument in Houston is 567 feet.
- The Washington Monument is 555 feet.
- Mount Rushmore is 500 feet.
- Perry's Victory and International Peace Memorial in Put-in-Bay, Ohio, is 352 feet.
- The Jefferson Davis Monument in Fairview, Kentucky, is 351 feet.
- The Statue of Liberty is 305 feet.
- Soldiers and Sailors Monument in Indianapolis is 284 feet.
- Bunker Hill Monument in Boston is 221 feet.
- Originally, the Gateway Arch was supposed to be 590 feet. When designer Eero Saarinen discovered the nearby Mansion House Apartments were going to be built at 300, he was concerned the Arch would lose its visual effect. Saarinen raised the Arch's height so it would be at least twice as tall as its neighbors.

Wright also called the Wainwright "height triumphant."

Wright's observation is echoed by Gwendolyn Wright, a professor of architecture at Columbia University, who said, "The thing about the Wainwright that is so extraordinary is that it's the first building to revel in height."

(And don't forget, two Wrights don't make a wrong.)

Three developments converged in the late nineteenth century resulting in taller buildings. The Wainwright Building came along at a time when urban space was scarce and developers seeking to expand had to look upward. Also, Sir Henry Bessemer had invented new ways to make steel, thus aiding the production of steel beams for tall buildings. Third, James Otis invented the elevator, which allowed upper floors to suddenly become much more accessible.

The Wainwright Building in St. Louis is heralded as one of the great buildings in the United States as evidenced by countless books on the subject. In New York, the Skyscraper Museum pays homage to the Wainwright by noting, "Though only ten stories, the Wainwright Building was one of the first high rises to clearly express verticality. Rather than composing the façade as a series of horizontal zones, Louis Sullivan emphasized the unbroken rise of the piers."

Wainwright Building.
Courtesy Library of Congress

The World's Tallest Human

In addition to tall buildings and monuments, the St. Louis area was also home to the world's tallest man.

Robert Wadlow of Alton, Illinois, stood at 8 feet 11 inches. Wadlow's height is a rare distinction when you consider 7 billion people currently occupy the planet. An estimated 107 billion people have lived on Earth, and no records indicate anyone was taller than Wadlow.

Wadlow was born with normal weight in 1918 but weighed forty-four pounds by the time he was one. Doctors knew Wadlow had an overactive pituitary gland but were unable to correct it. He was 7 feet 10 inches at age sixteen.

Aside from his height, Wadlow lived as normal a life as possible. When thirteen, he was a 7-foot 4-inch boy scout. He collected stamps and matchbooks. He enjoyed photography and joined the YMCA. He was a good student until college when he encountered difficulty working with pencils and lab equipment made for much smaller people. Also, his bones were weak and broke easily. Travel to class on ice was difficult. He abandoned his plans to become a lawyer and dropped out of school.

At twenty, Wadlow became a traveling spokesperson for the International Shoe Company. With his father, he visited more than 800 towns in 41 states as a goodwill representative for the company. People flocked to his appearances where he always left behind a pair of his size 37 shoes as a souvenir for the town and an advertisement for the company.

In Michigan, his feet developed blisters, which he could not feel due to a neurological disorder. As a result, infection set in. The infection spread, and Wadlow died on July 15, 1940.

Forty thousand people attended his funeral in Alton. Local businesses closed in observance of his death. Wadlow's parents buried him in a concrete vault to prevent anyone from tampering with his remains. His clothes were destroyed so they would never be put on display.

A statue of Robert Wadlow was erected in his honor in Alton in 1986.

Wally Moon–The Cardinal Who Gave Us the Term "Flake"

If someone is a flake, that person is a little nutty, off his rocker, weird, odd, a screwball, etc. The slang term came out of the St. Louis Cardinals organization. In 1956, Wally Moon referred to his teammate Jackie Brandt as a flake. Moon meant to say Brandt was so wild that his brains were falling out of his head, or flaking out of his head, and thus the term "flake."

Soon the word traveled around Major League Baseball circles. Teammates with eccentric behavior became flakes. *The Dickson Baseball Dictionary* says baseball's most notorious flakes included Brandt, of course, as well as Denny McLain, Phil Linz, Bill "Spaceman" Lee, Mark Fidrych, Jay Johnstone, Ross Grimsley, and Al "The Mad Hungarian" Hrabosky, now a Cardinals announcer. The term ended up in common usage in the 1960s and 1970s.

Gordon Jenkins Wrote "Folsom Prison Blues"

Gordon Jenkins, a top composer and arranger during the 1940s and 1950s, arranged Frank Sinatra's "It Was a Very Good Year" and Nat King Cole's "When I Fall in Love." He also wrote "Goodbye," which ended every Benny Goodman concert. Gordon Jenkins grew up in Webster Groves on Plant Avenue.

> It's almost a secret Jenkins also wrote the music and lyrics for Folsom Prison Blues, a signature tune for Johnny Cash, considered one of the top Country and Western songs of all time.

Because "Folsom" is so closely associated with Cash, people are shocked to learn of the St. Louis connection.

Here's the story: Gordon Jenkins wrote "Crescent City Blues" in 1953. It was sung by his wife, Beverly Mahr. Cash heard the song when he was in the Air Force in Germany and turned it into "Folsom Prison Blues," which appeared on his debut album *With His Hot and Blue Guitar* in 1957. When Cash performed the song on national television in 1969, Jenkins's friends went crazy.

"I'm watching Cash one night, singing this big record of his, and it's the biggest theft I ever heard," trumpeter Bruce Hudson recalled. "It was unbelievable the guts it took to do that. I called Gordon and said, 'What the hell is this?'"

Gordon's agent Harold Plant immediately filed suit. Cash paid Jenkins $75,000 to settle the matter.

In the mid-1990s, Cash told a Canadian magazine he developed "Folsom Prison Blues" when he was a nobody in the military. "At the time, I really had no idea I would be a professional recording artist; I wasn't trying to rip anybody off," he said. "So when I later went to Sun to record the song, I told Sam Phillips that I rewrote an old song to make my song, and that was that. Sometime later I met up with Gordon Jenkins and we talked about what had happened, and everything was right."

Charles Lindbergh

St. Louis produced the world's first modern media superstar in 1927 when twenty-five-year-old Charles Lindbergh flew across the Atlantic in the *Spirit of St. Louis* airplane. If you took Pope Francis, Lady Gaga, Prince William, and Barack Obama; added them all together; and then multiplied by ten, you would then approach the attention this unknown airmail pilot from St. Louis received when he became the first solo pilot to fly an airplane nonstop across the Atlantic from New York to Paris.

How big was Lindbergh as a superstar? Scott Berg chronicled the pilot's sudden fame in his Pulitzer Prize–winning biography, *Lindbergh*. A few examples:

With six hours notice, 150,000 fans showed up at Le Bourget Field in Paris to greet his flight. News of his accomplishment took up the entire front page and most of the next twenty pages of the *New York Times* the following day.

A French official said Lindbergh accomplished "the most audacious feat of the century."

Lindbergh received correspondence with praise from the president of Argentina, Pope Pius XI, and Mussolini. He received invitations to meet King George of England and King Albert of Belgium, which he accepted.

He was offered $5 million in endorsements, the equivalent of $65 million today, but he turned them all down. Before he returned to the United States, a dozen biographies of him were being prepared.

Back home, he met with President Calvin Coolidge and received the first-ever Distinguished Flying Cross. Then he dined with the Cabinet.

A postage stamp was issued in his honor, the first time for a living person.

Four million people turned out in New York City for his ticker-tape parade led by 10,000 soldiers and sailors. Nearly all schools and businesses, including the New York Stock Exchange, closed for the day. Cardinal Hayes of New York called him "the first and finest American boy of the day." Thirty-seven hundred guests joined Lindbergh at a dinner in his honor at the Hotel Commodore, a record for the hotel.

The next day all of Brooklyn was closed for Charles Lindbergh Day as another million people showed up to catch a glimpse of him in a twenty-two-mile parade.

More than 200 songs, hymns, and marches were written in his honor. The *New York Times* alone received more than 2,000 Lindbergh-inspired poems in a week.

When he returned to St. Louis, he was greeted by 3.5 million letters, 100,000 telegrams, and 14,000 parcels.

Paperboys in Springfield, Illinois, sent him a fountain pen for helping them sell more newspapers. The National League gave him a lifetime pass to all future baseball games.

He toured the world and was greeted by heads of state

Charles Lindbergh and the *Spirit of St. Louis*.
Courtesy Library of Congress

everywhere. He became the most photographed person on the planet.

He loaned his trophies to the Missouri History Museum. Eighty thousand people visited in the first week for the viewing. In the next eighteen months, another 1.5 million people would visit the museum to see them.

He immediately wrote a book detailing his adventure. A collector offered him $50,000 for the original manuscript—instead, he donated it to the Missouri History Museum in Forest Park.

Marquis Childs of the *St. Louis Post-Dispatch* wrote, "Five centuries have been required to make a saint of Joan of Arc but in two years Col. Charles A. Lindbergh has become a demigod."

But things turned awry. Lindbergh's every move was chronicled daily. Blueprints of his house were published, as were maps to his home. Newspapers printed his every move and itinerary.

Lindbergh's twenty-month-old baby was kidnapped and killed. The subsequent trial was dubbed "the trial of the century."

Later, Germany's Adolph Hitler gave a medal to Lindbergh, which was not returned during or after World War II despite the atrocities of Nazi Germany. This failure and his infamously anti-Semitic speech in Des Moines in September 1941 caused even greater controversy.

Lindbergh did inspect the German air force at the behest of the U.S. government. And Lindbergh flew fifty World War II combat missions—without wearing a uniform—for the United States, including the downing of a Japanese plane.

In his memoir, *The Spirit of St. Louis*, published in 1952, Lindbergh stated, "My greatest asset lies in the character of my partners in St. Louis."

Gert Cori: First American Woman to Win the Nobel Prize in Medicine

The first American woman to win the Nobel Prize in Medicine was a St. Louisan, Gerty Cori. Every schoolgirl knows that, right? Few if any do.

Gerty Theresa Radnitz was born in Prague in 1896. At age sixteen, she wanted to be a doctor, a rare profession for women of her day. To put this in context, in 1900 leading German neurologist Paul Julius Moebius had written a pamphlet *On the Physiological Feeblemindedness of Women*, claiming women were intellectually inferior to men because of their smaller brains. Ignoring Moebius, Cori took a crash course in pre-med studies, cramming Latin, math, and science in two years so she could begin medical school at age eighteen.

She earned her MD in 1920 and married fellow doctor Carl Cori the same year. The two decided to pursue biochemistry research instead of practicing medicine.

But life in Europe after World War I was difficult in many ways. Carl had to prove he was of Aryan descent to get a position at the University of Graz. Because Gerty was Jewish and a woman, her prospects of getting an academic position were difficult. In 1922, the Coris moved to Buffalo, New York, where they conducted research at the New York Institute for the Study of Malignant Diseases. They became U.S. citizens in 1928.

In America, the Coris learned it was "un-American" for wives to work with their husbands. In Buffalo, Carl became a biochemist while Gerty got an associate pathologist's job, a lesser position than her husband's despite their equivalent credentials. Three years later, they relocated to Washington University in St. Louis.

At Wash U, Gerty worked a research associate's job paying one-tenth of Carl's salary as full professor and department chair, even though, in the lab, they were equal partners. University rules at the time prohibited husbands and wives serving as concurrent faculty members.

In 1947, the Coris won the Nobel Prize in Medicine for discovering not only how glycogen is broken down in the body but also the enzyme responsible for it. The compound glucose-1-phosphate is now known as the "Cori-ester." No American woman had ever won the award. Speaking of namesakes, today the cycling of molecules in the liver, blood, and muscle cells is called the "Cori Cycle."

Not only did the Coris win the Nobel Prize, an astonishing six other scientists in their workplace later won Nobel Prizes, a feat unmatched in the United States. You might say their St. Louis lab was to biochemistry what the New York Yankees are to baseball. In fact, some credit the Coris for starting the field of biochemistry.

Although it took sixteen years, Gerty was made a full professor at Washington University in 1947, the same year she won the Nobel Prize.

Despite suffering from the rare bone marrow disease myelofibrosis, Gerty worked until her death in 1957. Carl died in 1984. Today, much of our understanding of carbohydrate metabolism is thanks to Gerty and Carl Cori.

The Cori Crater on the moon is named after Gerty. In addition, a play has been made about her life. It is named after the 1901 German pamphlet claiming women are intellectually inferior, *The Feeblemindedness of Women*.

First Vice President to Get Married While in Office

On November 18, 1949, Alben W. Barkley, age seventy-one, wedded Jane Rucker Hadley, thirty-eight, at St. John's Methodist Church in St. Louis. Barkley became the first vice president to get married while in office.

The four-month courtship began on July 8, 1949, at the Washington home of President Harry S. Truman's special counsel Clark Clifford, who introduced the couple to each other. Barkley's first wife had died in 1947. Hadley's husband, a St. Louis lawyer for the Wabash Railroad, died in 1945.

Only thirty-three people—mostly family members—attended the nine-minute wedding ceremony. President Truman was not among them. Thousands gathered outside the Central West End church and backed up onto the steps of Temple Israel across the street. One woman fainted.

After the short ceremony, the couple headed outside to the "getaway" car, an automobile borrowed from St. Louis Mayor Joseph Darst. The enthusiastic well-wishers were barely controlled by thirty-five uniformed St. Louis police officers, twenty-five detectives, and fourteen boy scouts. Yes, that's correct: the vice president of the United States, one heartbeat away from being the leader of the free world, was guarded by boy scouts.

The newlyweds, engulfed by the crowd, had difficulty getting into their vehicle. According to an account in the *St. Louis Post-Dispatch*, police pushed back against the pressing spectators. An officer eventually opened the car's door and his colleagues formed a wedge to clear a path for the exiting vehicle through the throngs of onlookers. After the Barkleys departed, women from the crowd hurried into the church to take the wedding's flower decorations as souvenirs.

The wedding reception took place immediately afterward at the home of Mrs. T. M. Sayman, 5399 Lindell Boulevard, for a wedding luncheon of lobster newberg, turkey, ham, green string beans with sliced pecans, mushrooms with pimentos, corn cranberries, rolls, chef's salad, and sherbet. The luncheon, as well as the earlier scene outside the church, was broadcast live by the NBC-TV network.

Following the luncheon, Mrs. Barkley and the vice president—with Mrs. Barkley at the wheel—drove away in an Oldsmobile convertible, her wedding gift from her new husband.

President Truman shakes hands with Vice President Alben Barkley as he presents him with a gold medal for distinguished service in Congress. Jane Barkley is to the left. Courtesy National Archives and Records Administration

7Up–A Native St. Louisan

The soft drink 7Up traces its roots to 1920 when St. Louisan C. L. Grigg of the Howdy Corporation (not making that up) produced an orange beverage called Howdy. Even though Howdy was a popular drink consumed across the nation, Grigg kept attempting to improve its taste. He wanted a drink with a distinctive flavor that effectively quenched thirsts.

Formulas were created and discarded. A dozen bottlers made different variations, bottled them, took criticism, and reported the results. After twelve different combinations of lemons, limes, and carbonated water, in 1929 Grigg finally came up with a thirteenth soda he called Bib-Label Lithiated Lemon-Lime Soda (not making this up either).

He later changed the name to 7Up. Nobody knows to this day what the heck this name was supposed to mean! The first franchised bottler was the Seven-Up Bottling Company of St. Louis.

Although it made its debut alongside the Stock Market Crash of 1929 and spent its adolescent years in the Great Depression, 7Up survived. It was so successful the Howdy Corpo-

The Almighty Twinkie

What famous food was inspired by a St. Louis billboard? The Twinkie. Its inventor, James A. Dewar, came up with the name for the cream-filled sponge cake after seeing a billboard here in 1930 for "Twinkle Toe Shoes."

ration changed its name to the Seven-Up Company in 1937. By the 1940s, it was the third best-selling soft drink in the world.

By 1964, St. Louis's Seven-Up Co. was parent company to about six hundred bottlers in the United States and Canada. 7Up was sold in 2 million locations. It introduced an "uncola" ad campaign in 1967 and soon uncola was a household word.

In 1978, Seven-Up was sold to cigarette maker Phillip Morris and has since been owned at various times by Dr. Pepper, Cadbury Schweppes, and Snapple.

The Birthplace of Puffed Rice

Many St. Louisans accept as dogma the St. Louis World's Fair in 1904 introduced the ice cream cone, iced tea, and hot dogs to the world. However, author Pamela J. Vaccaro has proven all three concoctions were consumed before 1904.

So, was any food introduced to the world in St. Louis in 1904?

Yes: puffed rice.

According to Vaccaro, St. Louis is the home of puffed rice. The Quaker Oats exhibit at the 1904 World's Fair in St. Louis shot puffed rice out of canons every fifty minutes. Although the Anderson Puffed Rice Company, a division of Quaker Oats, had invented puffed rice in 1903, they introduced it to the world in Forest Park in 1904. It does not appear fairgoers ate it as cereal with milk. Instead, early puffed rice was caramelized and sold in boxes.

John Colter: First to See Yellowstone, and Much More

The most athletic and daring person in the history of St. Louis is likely someone most people have never heard of: John Colter.

After Lewis and Clark returned to St. Louis in 1806, fur traders sought members of the Corps of Discovery to help trap beaver and work with Indians. St. Louis fur trader Manuel Lisa hired Corps member John Colter.

In 1807 and 1808, Colter walked about 500 miles by himself with a thirty-pound backpack through what is now Idaho, Montana, and Wyoming. Historian Hiram M. Chittenden called Colter "the first explorer of the Valley of the Bighorn River; the first to cross the passes of the head of Wind River and see the deadwaters of the Colorado of the West; the first to see the Teton Mountains, Jackson Hole, Pierre's Hole and the sources of the Snake river; and most important of all, the first to pass through that singular region which has since become known throughout the world as the Yellowstone Wonderland."

> According to historian Eric Jay Dolan, it was without a doubt one of the most impressive solo journeys in American exploration history.

That would seem to wrap up the chapter on John Colter, right? What, after that journey, could John possibly do for an encore?

Well, later in 1808, Colter was sent to escort Crow and Flathead Indians to Fort Manuel at the confluence of the Yellowstone and Bighorn rivers. The mission was dangerous because the Crow and Flathead tribes were rivals to the Blackfeet Indians who populated the area. Relations between Americans and Blackfeet were frayed since the Lewis and Clark expedition killed two Blackfeet attempting to steal horses and rifles in 1806.

Colter was attacked by the Blackfeet. Although wounded, he managed to shoot his way out of trouble, and the Blackfeet retreated.

Later that year, Colter was attacked again by Blackfeet, this time at the so-called Three Forks area at the confluence of the Jefferson, Madison, and Gallatin rivers. Along with his partner John Potts, another Corps alum, Colter was surrounded by 500 to 600 Blackfeet.

When Potts tried to escape, he was hit by an arrow. He fired back with his rifle. The Blackfeet responded with arrows in torrents, killing Potts. The Blackfeet apprehended Colter, stripped him naked, and asked if he could run. Colter told his captors he was a slow runner. Giving Colter a lead of about 400 yards, the chief released Colter and told him to run for his life. With bare feet, no clothing, and hundreds of Indians at his back, Colter took off. Prickly pears and stones ripped the skin on his feet.

A lone Indian, at one point about twenty yards behind and gaining, almost caught Colter. But Colter turned around suddenly, caught the man off balance, and, after killing him with his own spear, ran on. When other Indians caught up to find their comrade's body, they grew more enraged.

Colter made it to a river and hid under a collection of trees and brushwood in the water. Indians paced the area for several hours, at times walking on logs just above Colter's head at the water's surface. Finally, the Blackfeet moved on.

What was Colter to do? *According to Dolin, he walked naked for seven days over 250 miles!* He survived by eating local vegetation and arrived, barely alive, at Fort Manuel where he regained his health.

He died of disease, perhaps typhus, in 1812 or 1813, depending on the account. Some say Colter was buried in the cemetery at Fee Fee Baptist Church in Bridgeton, but no tombstone has been found. Others indicate he was buried in Dundee, Missouri, in a cemetery later removed for a railroad. Today, John Colter running races are held annually in Driggs, Idaho, and Bozeman, Montana.

The First Interstate

Lewis and Clark returned to St. Louis from their twenty-eight month trek to the Pacific Northwest in 1806. A century and a half later, St. Louis travelers would achieve another historic milestone.

The Federal-Aid Highway Act of 1956 "paved the way" for our nation's interstate highway system. This bill funded the Interstate Construction Program, which financed construction, set design standards, and commenced the national commitment to efficient highway transportation.

The first project to go to construction with federal highway funds under this program was in St. Charles County.

On August 13, 1956, work began there on I-70, sometimes known as the Mark Twain Expressway.

Today, I-70 stretches 2,100 miles between Baltimore, Maryland, and Cove Fort, Utah. If Lewis and Clark made their journey by automobile using the U.S. Interstate System, they could have completed the round-trip within three days.

Lyon: A Military First

In May of 1861, one month after the fall of Fort Sumter and the beginning of the Civil War, President Abraham Lincoln assigned Captain Nathaniel Lyon as commander of the Unionists in St. Louis. At the same time, Missouri Governor Claiborne Jackson, loyal to the South, ordered militia companies into training under the direction of General Daniel M. Frost.

Lyon was concerned the militia would attempt to seize the city's arsenal with its "sixty thousand Springfield and Enfield rifles, 1.5 million cartridges, ninety thousand pounds of powder, and artillery pieces." According to historian James Neal Primm, the St. Louis Arsenal was the largest military storehouse in any of the slave states, and the Confederacy wanted it.

On May 9, Captain Lyon decided to personally inspect Frost's camp, located at Lindell Grove near Grand Avenue and Olive Street. Borrowing a bombazine gown and veil from the mother-in-law of

General Nathaniel Lyon.
Courtesy Library of Congress

Frank Blair, a St. Louis attorney loyal to President Lincoln, Lyon disguised himself as a woman. Riding in a carriage through the camp—dubbed Camp Jackson—Lyon noticed a street sign marked "Jeff Davis." Convinced of the militia's rebel sympathies and its possible attack on the arsenal, Lyon mustered 6,000 troops on May 10 and closed the camp.

It was the first and perhaps last instance in U.S. military history of a cross-dressing military commander.

Frost Campus

Years later, Saint Louis University occupied the area once known as Camp Jackson. General Frost's daughter Harriet donated $1,050,000 to the school in 1959, and the area is now known as the Frost Campus. The contribution came with one condition: the statue of Nathaniel Lyon at the intersection of Grand Avenue and West Pine Street had to be moved. Today, it stands across town in what is now Lyon Park at the foot of Arsenal Street.

A First U.S. Summer Olympics

This book is *Amazing St. Louis* and, as its author, I am obligated to tell stories about the people and events of St. Louis that were, well, amazing. Of course, amazing can be good or bad. And in some cases, it can be odd or bizarre. That describes the 1904 Olympic Marathon in St. Louis.

First, it must be said it is amazing St. Louis was home to the 1904 Summer Olympic Games. Only two other U.S. cities have hosted the Summer Olympics: Atlanta and Los Angeles (twice). Chicago? Nope. New York? No. San Francisco? No. No. No.

So, just having held the games is quite a distinction for St. Louis. However, the 1904 Olympic Marathon was amazing in a bizarre way. It was chockablock with oddities.

Where do we begin?

How about with St. Louis Olympics organizer James Sullivan allowing only two water stations on the 24.85-mile route. He wanted to study the effects of "purposeful dehydration." And denying water to marathoners would pretty much be the way to do it. No, he was not sued and jailed, as far as I know.

Also, the marathon did not start during a cooler part of the day, like 7 a.m., as most do today. It started at 3:03 p.m. on August 30. Temps and humidity soared into the 90s. If you have not been to St. Louis in August, let me just say it feels like a sauna . . . in Calcutta.

Ireland native John Lorden, winner of the 1903 Boston Marathon, dropped out of the race after about five minutes due to a vomiting fit. Why did Lorden get sick? Perhaps he could not handle the exhaust, fumes, and dust generated by the vehicles preceding the runners. Remember, this was before catalytic converters, air pollution controls, and paved roads.

William Garcia of California also dropped out and almost dropped dead. The automobile smoke covered his esophagus and ripped his stomach lining.

The contest was all the more difficult because many of the thirty-two competitors were unprepared for the distance; Greece sent ten runners, but none had ever run a marathon before. Plus, runners had to "dodge cross-town traffic, delivery wagons, railroad trains, trolley cars and people walking their dogs." Even two race-course officials were severely injured after their car veered off the road when they tried to avoid hitting a runner.

Len Tau and Jan Mashiani, from the Tsuana tribe of South Africa, ran the race in their bare feet—quite an endeavor considering the roads were mostly stone and dirt. They finished ninth and twelfth, respectively. Tau might have fared better if a dog hadn't chased him off the side of the road.

Mailman Felix Carvajal of Cuba lost all his money gambling in New Orleans before arriving in St. Louis. He hitched a ride to Missouri and showed up at the starting line in long dark pants and a white dress shirt with long sleeves. He asked people on the route for fruit. When denied food, he took a group's peaches and ran. Carvajal got sick eating rotten apples he picked from a tree along the course. Unable to proceed, he lay down on the roadside and took a nap. He eventually got up and finished fourth.

Felix Carvajal. Courtesy Library of Congress

Fred Lorz, a bricklayer from New York, qualified for the race by running a modest five-mile trial. He quit the marathon after the ninth mile and rode in a car until the nineteenth. There, he got out and began running along the route. When Lorz entered the stadium, he was greeted by cheers from the crowd of 10,000. The daughter of the president of the United States, Alice Roosevelt, took a photo with him and almost awarded him the gold medal. Others intervened, and Lorz immediately acknowledged he was not the winner.

The winner was Thomas Hicks of Cambridge who suffered from severe dehydration, losing eight of his 133 pounds in the race. During the marathon, his coaches gave him strychnine (a pesticide, and I am not making this up either), egg whites, and brandy. He collapsed when it was his turn to receive the gold medal. Four doctors worked to revive him, and when they did, he retired from marathoning.

The First African-American Olympian(s)

George Poage of the Milwaukee Athletic Club was the first African-American to compete in the Olympics. At the 1904 Olympics in St. Louis, Poage ran in the 60-meter dash on Monday August 29. He came in fourth place in his heat and did not advance to the finals.

It was assumed for many years Poage was the only black athlete competing in 1904 and thus the first African-American medalist. In the book *Olympic Games: 1904*, track official Charles J. P. Lucas said, "Poage was the colored sprinter from the Milwaukee Athletic Club, the only colored man to compete in the games."

However, scholars later determined Joseph Stadler of the Franklin Athletic Club in Cleveland was also African-American. The reason his racial identity was kept a secret or misidentified is unknown. In any event, on Wednesday, August 31, 1904, both Poage and Stadler competed in the 400-meter hurdles and standing high jump, respectively. Poage took home a bronze and Stadler won a silver.

Thus, Poage and Stadler are the first African-American athletes to medal at the Olympic Games, and they did so in St. Louis.

After the Olympics, Poage taught at Sumner High School in St. Louis.

The First Jewish Justice

The first Jewish justice of the U.S. Supreme Court, Louis Brandeis, was admitted to the bar inside the Old Courthouse in downtown St. Louis. He held his first job as an attorney in the 500 block of Chestnut Street. Brandeis came to St. Louis after graduating from Harvard Law School in 1877. He grew restless in St. Louis and returned to Boston less than a year later.

Brandeis, who developed a form of legal opinion writing known today as the "Brandeis brief," served on the U.S. Supreme Court from 1916 until 1939.

Louis Brandeis. Courtesy Library of Congress

Section Two

St. Louisans Who Changed the World

Chuck Berry Invented Rock and Roll

Of all the stories in this book, this one perplexes me the most. I just don't understand why St. Louis generally fails to recognize how rock and roll, the most important art form of the second half of the twentieth century, is a local creation.

The rest of the world keeps telling us if there is an inventor of rock, it's a St. Louisan. Other cities would jump up and down bragging about this. St. Louis could, but doesn't. Anyhow, here is what others say:

Rolling Stone magazine, the bible of rock music, declared in 2010, "Fifty-five years ago, Chuck Berry invented rock and roll."

The Rolling Stones' Keith Richards, of undisputed rock bona fides, put it this way at Berry's induction ceremony in the Rock and Roll Hall of Fame in 1986: "It's very difficult for me to talk about Chuck Berry 'cause I've lifted every lick he ever played—this is the gentleman who started it all."

John Lennon of the Beatles said, "If you tried to give rock and roll another name, you might call it 'Chuck Berry.'"

In 1926, Berry was born at 2520 Goode Avenue—his humongous hit "Johnny B. Goode" is named after the street—and he has lived and performed in St. Louis his entire life.

Berry was in the first class inducted into the Rock and Roll Hall of Fame. His plaque there states, "While no individual can be said to have invented rock and roll, Chuck Berry arguably did more than anyone else to put the pieces together."

So, a guy who has lived and worked in St. Louis all his life is credited by the most respected rock sources to have come up with rock and roll. As someone who grew up elsewhere, I find that very impressive and amazing.

You already have enough information to pass Chuck Berry 101. Here is some additional information for you grad students.

Berry influenced other rock bands who would become the most influential artists in rock.

Lennon's Beatles recorded Berry's "Roll Over Beethoven" and made it the opening track of their second album.

The Beatles also performed Berry's "Rock and Roll Music" on their 1964 tour.

Their song "Come Together" includes lyrics ("Here come old flattop, he come grooving up slowly") very similar to Berry's "You Can't Catch Me" ("Here come a flat-top, he was movin' up with me").

Chuck Berry performs at Blueberry Hill. Courtesy Blueberry Hill

In October 1961 in Dartford, England, eighteen-year-old Mick Jagger, a student at the London School of Economics, caught the eye of seventeen-year-old Keith Richards because of the album he was carrying: *Rockin' at the Hops* by Chuck Berry. The two would form a friendship and the Rolling Stones.

The Rolling Stones' first single? "Come On," by Chuck Berry. The Stones' second album included another Berry tune, "You Can't Catch Me."

Of Berry, Keith Richards later wrote, "I could never overstress how important he was in my development."

The Beach Boys are also one of the most iconic (overused word but quite appropriate here) and influential rock groups. Who influenced them? Well, their 1963 hit "Surfin' U.S.A." used the melody and rhythm of Berry's "Sweet Little Sixteen." Berry was later given a songwriting credit for the song. In addition, the opening guitar lick of the Beach Boys' "Fun, Fun, Fun" is the same as Berry's opening of "Johnny B. Goode."

Joe Perry of Aerosmith summed it up best, "If you want to learn rock and roll, you have to learn Chuck Berry."

What if the whole world—except for St. Louis—recognized St. Louis as a great baseball town? That's kind of what we have going on with the Chuck Berry–St. Louis connection.

I look at it this way: since rock and roll came from Chuck Berry, and Chuck Berry has always lived in St. Louis, therefore, "rock and roll came from St. Louis!" Let the word go forth.

U.S. Grant Saves the Union . . . Twice

Ulysses S. Grant met and married his wife, Julia, in St. Louis. They lived here when he returned from military service in 1854. His home is now a historic site run by the National Park Service. A part of his nineteenth-century farm is preserved at Grant's Farm, a tourist attraction. A statue of Grant stands in front of the St. Louis City Hall.

May St. Louisans brag about Grant as Bostonians embrace Paul Revere and Philadelphians behold Ben Franklin?

Most definitely.

U.S. Grant 1868 election pin. Courtesy Library of Congress

Grant saved the Union not once but *twice*, according to Pulitzer Prize–finalist H. W. Brands. First, as supreme commander of the Union armies in the Civil War, Grant racked up victories from the Battle of Fort Henry in 1862 to the defeat of Robert E. Lee's Army of Northern Virginia in April 1865. When Lee surrendered to Grant at Appomattox Court House, Grant had "defeated secession and destroyed slavery, secession's cause."

That was the first time Grant saved the Union. The second time?

As president, Grant guided the nation through the turbulent years of post–Civil War Reconstruction. His Enforcement Acts of 1870–71 broke the power of the Ku Klux Klan, which threatened to throw the South into chaos. In the White House, he pursued Lincoln's goal of reuniting the country and bringing former slaves into one indivisible nation. Grant shepherded the South back into the Union when it could have fallen into anarchy.

According to Brands, when Grant left office, the United States "was more secure than at any previous time in the history of the nation. And no one had done more to produce that result than he."

Conclusion of Brands, a professor at the University of Texas? A St. Louisan saved the nation's bacon twice.

Dred Scott: The Lawsuit That Led to the Civil War

Did a St. Louisan cause the Civil War?

In 1846, the slaves Dred and Harriet Scott sued for their freedom in the Old Courthouse in St. Louis. Dred Scott contended that when his master took him to a free state he ceased to be a slave. Two trials were held in St. Louis. The Scotts won one and lost one. Eventually, the case appeared in front of the Supreme Court of the United States in 1857.

The Supreme Court justices ruled 7–2 that Scott should remain a slave. But Supreme Court Chief Justice Roger B. Taney, writing the "majority opinion" for the court, went further. He ruled Dred Scott, a black man, was not a citizen of the United States and had no right to sue in federal courts. Taney also ruled Scott was never free in the territories, and the Missouri Compromise banning slavery in the territories was unconstitutional.

Public outcry against the decision, at least in the North, was intense.

Dred Scott. Courtesy Library of Congress

Considered by some the most infamous case in Supreme Court history, the Dred Scott decision led to sectional conflict, the Lincoln-Douglas debates, and the election of Abraham Lincoln, which divided the nation.

Like a spark that results in a forest fire, this St. Louis lawsuit led to the Civil War!

After the decision, ownership of the Scotts reverted to the Blow family, who had once owned them and provided financial assistance during their legal struggle. The Blows freed the Scotts in May of 1857. Dred Scott died of tuberculosis fifteen months later.

As if the substance of the ruling was not controversial enough, the name of Dred Scott's owner, the defendant John Sanford, was incorrectly spelled "Sandford" in the court documents and Taney opinion. Now, you would think when a case reaches the highest court in the land someone would check this stuff but, no, even the Supreme Court can make typos.

Harry Blackmun: From Hot Sauna to Hot Decisions

St. Louis has a connection to yet another famous Supreme Court decision: *Roe v. Wade.* Harry Blackmun, the Supreme Court justice who wrote the landmark 1973 decision, lived at the Missouri Athletic Club (MAC) in downtown St. Louis when President Richard Nixon appointed him to the Court on April 14, 1970.

An athletic club might seem a strange place for a judge to live. Blackmun lived most of the year in Rochester, Minnesota, and stayed in St. Louis while serving on the 8th Circuit Court of Appeals. The MAC provided hotel rooms, a restaurant, and a workout area. Former MAC Athletic Director Dan Barks remembers Blackmun "using the club's fifth floor steam room and sauna."

However, the judge's residence would *not* be his biggest surprise. At the time of his elevation to the high court, Blackmun told the *St. Louis Post-Dispatch,* "I've been a Republican all my life." A colleague describing Blackmun said, "He usually follows precedent."

The day he was nominated, Blackmun was called a "strict constructionist in his interpretation of the constitution." Sounds as expected—after all, he was the nominee of a Republican president, right?

Three years later, Justice Harry Blackmun changed the American legal landscape for women. He granted constitutional protection for abortion by writing *Roe v. Wade,* later described as one of the Court's most liberal, historic, and controversial decisions of the century!

The Kid from Webster Groves Who Ended the Cold War

William H. Webster served as a judge in St. Louis, both on the federal bench in the Eastern District of Missouri and on the 8th Circuit Court of Appeals. Then Judge Webster was offered the job as director of the FBI.

"I talked to the Chief Justice Warren Burger who thought (taking the FBI directorship) would be a dead end job for me," Webster later recalled. "But then I talked to Wade McCree, a distinguished former judge on the 6th Circuit who was solicitor general, and he said, 'This is not a duty but if you want to make a patriotic gift to your country, I can't think of a better one.'"

Webster took the job and became just the third permanent chief of the bureau, following J. Edgar Hoover and Clarence M. Kelley. All this success came from an idyllic childhood in suburban Webster Groves.

How was growing up in Webster Groves? "Wonderful," according to Webster. "I was a child of the Depression as were all the other kids at that time. We maintained a top-drawer school system. We played a lot of baseball and tennis. Country clubs were out of the question for us, but we didn't care and we didn't know the difference."

As a kid, Webster stayed busy. "I had scouting and all sorts of activities outside of school. We never thought of ourselves as poor. And our fathers got us the best education: 85 percent of our class at Webster High went to college, and 15 percent went east on scholarships—as I did." Webster went from Webster Groves High School to Amherst College, followed by the naval reserves and Washington University Law School.

On March 4, 1987, as Webster was about to become the next director of Central Intelligence, the *New York Times* opined, "In 9 years since his arrival in Washington, Mr. Webster, a former federal judge, is seen as having largely restored the reputation of the FBI."

As CIA director, Webster helped the Afghan rebels take on the invading Soviets. "I didn't invent the idea," he admitted. "I give (former CIA Director) Bill Casey credit for meeting Russian imperialism around the world. (Arming the Afghan rebels) was uniquely successful. We did not operate in Afghanistan. We did most of our work in Pakistan where we were allowed to train the (Afghan) Mujahideen and the tribes, who were, for a change, all united in their common desire to get the Russians out of their country."

CIA involvement in Afghanistan under Webster's leadership in the late 1980s proved to be a crucial move in ending Soviet power. "As a result, the Russians left. Their army was humiliated. The Warsaw Pact countries were less impressed with Soviet might and began to act independently. It accelerated the end of the Cold War—in our favor."

In sum, the Berlin Wall fell and the Soviet Union dissolved as a result of the policy employed by William Webster as director of the Central Intelligence Agency. Not a bad legacy for the Depression-era kid from Webster Groves.

The Only Person to Be Director of Both the FBI and the CIA

When Webster became director of Central Intelligence, he appeared on the cover of *Time* magazine on March 16, 1987. This St. Louisan became the first and last person in U.S. history to hold the top positions at both the FBI and CIA.

C. V. Riley Saves the French Wine Industry

As far as I'm concerned, all St. Louisans should be able to drink free wine in Paris. After all, if not for one St. Louisan, there would be no French wine.

In the nineteenth century, a pest destroyed 2½ million acres—about one-third—of French vineyards. The louse ate the roots of grape vines. The French tried hundreds of ways to rid their country of the insect. None proved successful.

In 1870, Charles V. Riley, an English-born state entomologist working in St. Louis, identified the pest as the grape *phylloxera*. He also discovered a North American grapevine—*Vitis labrusca*—resistant to this insect. He suggested grafting European grapes to the *Vitis labrusca* rootstock.

These trials were conducted in St. Louis and at two other Missouri nurseries. They proved to be the only reliable way to end the grape devastation in France. By 1880, millions of vines and cuttings were sent from Missouri to France. The French hailed the entomologist in St. Louis for saving their wine industry. Riley was awarded the French Grand Gold Medal and was named a Chevalier of the Legion of Honor in 1884.

Sadly, Riley later moved to Washington, D.C., where he died in 1895 in a bicycle accident. However, this St. Louisan's legacy lives wherever a bottle of French wine is opened.

SAVE MARIA

On May 21, 1972, Laszlo Toth, a thirty-three-year-old Hungarian geologist, set out to destroy the great Michelangelo's *Pietà*, one of the world's most famous religious sculptures. Located in St. Peter's Basilica in Rome, the sculpture depicts the Virgin Mary holding the lifeless body of Jesus in her arms. Michelangelo created it in 1499.

According to *Time* magazine, Toth climbed over a guardrail and yelled, "I am Jesus Christ!" Using a hammer, he struck at the marble sculpture, chipping Mary's left eyelid, neck, head, and veil and breaking her left forearm.

Before Toth could inflict further damage, St. Louisan Bob Cassilly, a twenty-three-year-old Fontbonne College graduate in Rome on his honeymoon, jumped over the rail and lunged at Toth. "I leaped up and grabbed the guy by the beard," recalled Cassilly. "We both fell into the crowd of screaming Italians. It was somewhat of a scene." Cassilly "landed at least one punch on Toth" before being joined by a group of men who wrestled with Toth until security arrived.

In the melee, it is hard to say what might have happened if the quick-thinking St. Louisan had not acted. The world might have lost one of its greatest artistic treasures!

Pietà was repaired and is now protected by bulletproof glass.

Du Sable: Founder of Chicago

Visitors to Chicago notice a handsome monument and plaque on Michigan Avenue paying tribute to the city's first permanent resident, Jean Baptiste Point du Sable. Du Sable, half French and half African, was born in what is now Haiti around 1745. He made his way to New Orleans and then to Indiana, where he was a trader.

Harassed by both British and American troops—perhaps because of his color—du Sable moved to the Chicago River and established a fur trading post, thus becoming the first non-Indian settler of Chicago and its first black resident. The Indians said, "The first white man we knew was black."

The Chicago plaque indicates du Sable established his trading post in the early 1780s. Another plaque placed in 1912 at the corner of Pine and Kinzie streets in Chicago marks the spot of Chicago's first home, built by du Sable. However, the plaques fail to mention that du Sable sold his Chicago property in 1800 and moved to St. Charles, Missouri. In St. Charles, he lived at Second and Decatur streets until his death in 1818. Du Sable was buried in St. Charles Borromeo Cemetery.

Both Chicago and St. Charles honored the pioneer. A high school in Chicago was named after du Sable, and he was also one of eight individuals selected to be included in the frieze of the Illinois Centennial Building in 1965. A public park in St. Charles is named after him.

Here is the key point of the du Sable story all St. Louisans need to know and tell: even the founder of Chicago, in the end, decided he'd rather live in Cardinal Nation!

A Man Buried in St. Louis Sparked the American Revolution

Today, Pontiac is best known as a car, a stadium, or a city in Michigan. But the original Pontiac was a member of the Ottawa tribe. Like other Ottawas, Pontiac—born in 1720—enjoyed a good relationship with French settlers in the Great Lakes region who often provided Indians with gifts like food and ammunition.

When France lost American territory to Great Britain in the 1760s, the Ottawa and other tribes were forced to deal with the British. Unlike the French, the British had little use for gift giving. Or Indians. When poor relations with the British did not improve, Pontiac organized a mighty alliance of tribes to fight them. The Huron, Miami, Delaware, Chippewa, Kickapoo, Shawnee, Potawatomi, Seneca, and others united under Pontiac.

This coalition was the greatest confederation of tribes against white expansion in North America. British forts fell one by one. In all, the tribes captured eight forts and forced the British to abandon a ninth. However, royal powers back in Europe doomed the uprising. The French and British signed a peace treaty in the summer of 1763, which took the French, an important ally for Pontiac, out of the fighting.

Many of Pontiac's Indian allies abandoned the cause. Pontiac kept his own siege on Fort Detroit for six months, but his strength began to wane. The movement crumbled, and Pontiac agreed to peace with the British in 1765.

Although Pontiac's uprising had failed, his defiance changed the world. In London, King George viewed Pontiac's surprising successes as a sign his colonies were in danger and unable to

The Death of Pontiac, by De Cost Smith. Courtesy Library of Congress

defend themselves. He decided to send troops for protection. The king and Parliament also decided to tax the colonists to pay for the troops. Why, they asked, should the English pay for America's defense?

Thus, taxes were levied on the colonists, beginning with the Stamp Act in 1765. Britain required taxes on a variety of papers and documents produced in the colonies, including newspapers. This was the first direct tax imposed on the Americans. Of course, the tax resulted in an uproar in the colonies. "Taxation without representation" became the cry of the American Revolution and one of the principal British offenses listed in the Declaration of Independence.

Pontiac, meanwhile, began living a nomadic life. During a 1769 visit to the settlement of Cahokia in Illinois, he was murdered by a member of another tribe. Motives are unknown. His remains were transported to St. Louis and buried at the current site of the Stadium East Garage at the corner of Broadway and Walnut. (Yes, Pontiac lies beneath Hondas and Buicks!) A plaque at the downtown St. Louis site memorializes Pontiac's contributions to United States history and recognizes the man who sought independence from the British before the colonists themselves.

Historians may wonder: What if Pontiac had not fought the British? Would there have been a Stamp Act? Would there have been an American Revolution? The answers have been buried in St. Louis for 250 years.

Earl Weaver Pioneers the Radar Gun

Today, the speed of the pitch in Major League Baseball is noted almost as often as the ball and strike count. However, that was not always the case.

Earl Weaver, a native St. Louisan who attended Beaumont High School, was the first Major League manager to use the radar gun. "I was the first person to use it," Weaver admitted. "An old Cardinals left fielder Danny Litwhiler was coaching baseball at Michigan State University. They were in Florida playing in a tournament. He called me and said, 'I've got something I want you to see.'"

It was a radar gun. "I asked him, 'What's it used for?'

> Early in Earl Weaver's baseball career, he worked for the city of St. Louis in the off-season. In the winter of 1952, he installed parking meters. In other years, he sent out real estate and personal property tax bills while working in City Hall.
>
> "I guess I made a lot of enemies," Weaver later recalled.

"He said, 'Almost anything you want. You can tell if a pitcher's changeup is slow enough or if he's throwing it too hard. You can tell how fast a pitcher is.'

"I was managing the Orioles, and every scout would say about a prospect, 'This guy's throwing as hard as Jim Palmer.'" Then I'd look at the player, and he couldn't brake a pane of glass.

"I thought, 'Well, this radar gun will cut all that baloney.'

"I could also judge an outfielder's arm. You could do almost anything. I brought it up to the Orioles organization. They thought it was silly at first. But everyone carries one around now."

From Baby Teeth to Nuclear Test Ban: The St. Louis Baby Tooth Survey

St. Louis mothers—and their babies—helped frame the debate leading to an international treaty.

Starting in 1958, a group of St. Louis researchers known as the Committee for Nuclear Information asked parents to contribute their children's first teeth for a study called the St. Louis Baby Tooth Survey. Moms responded with enthusiasm: 325,000 baby teeth were collected!

Scientists at Washington University and Saint Louis University tested the teeth and determined they contained the radioactive isotope strontium-90, a byproduct of nuclear weapons testing.

Strontium-90 did not exist in the teeth of previous generations. Why?

There was no strontium-90 on earth until the explosion of the atomic bomb and subsequent testing of nuclear weapons after World War II.

Scientists determined the fallout from nuclear explosions was carried by wind and rain into the ground, then into grass eaten by cows, and finally into the bones and teeth of children who drank milk. The study found St. Louis children born after 1963 had fifty times as much strontium-90 as children born in 1950.

The St. Louis Baby Tooth Survey attracted a lot of press attention throughout the nation on TV, radio, and in newspapers. Eric Reiss, one of the study's leaders, testified before the Joint Congressional Committee on Atomic Energy in June 1963.

By July of 1963, the United States, Great Britain, and the Soviet Union agreed to a Nuclear Test Ban Treaty banning the testing of nuclear weapons in the air, underwater, and in outer space.

Addressing the nation on July 26, 1963, President John F. Kennedy expressed fear over the effects of nuclear testing on children's health:

> ". . . this treaty can be a step towards freeing the world from the fears and dangers of radioactive fallout . . . over the years the number and the yield of weapons tested have rapidly increased and so have the radioactive hazards from such testing. Continued unrestricted testing by the nuclear powers . . . will increasingly contaminate the air that all of us must breathe.
>
> "Even then, the number of children and grandchildren with cancer in their bones, with leukemia in their blood, or with poison in their lungs might seem statistically small to some, in comparison with natural health hazards. But this is not a natural health hazard—and it is not a statistical issue. The loss of even one human life, or the malformation of even one baby—who may be born long after we are gone—should be of concern to us all. Our children and grandchildren are not merely statistics toward which we can be indifferent."

The Senate ratified the test ban treaty by a vote of 80–19. President Kennedy signed it on October 7, 1963.

One year later in October 1964, President Lyndon Johnson recognized the St. Louis Baby Tooth Survey when he praised the treaty:

> "The treaty has halted the steady menacing increase in radioactive fallout. The deadly products of atomic explosions were poisoning our soil and our food and the milk our children drank and the air we breathe. Radioactive deposits were being formed in increasing quantity in the teeth and bones of young Americans."

The Nuclear Test Ban Treaty of 1963 is still in effect today.

Did the Mexican Revolution Have Roots in St. Louis?

Before that question is answered, a little background is helpful.

Porfirio Diaz served as president of Mexico for thirty-four years, from 1876 to 1911. During the Diaz years, Mexico's economy grew and its infrastructure improved, partly thanks to U.S. investment in rails and businesses. However, many Mexicans questioned their country's inequality, treatment of women, press restrictions, etc.

In 1900, Enrique Flores Magon and his brother Ricardo Flores Magon published *Regeneracion*, a liberal newspaper in Mexico. The paper criticized the Diaz government for corruption, miscarriages of justice, and violations of rights. In 1901, the government struck back by arresting the Magon brothers and imprisoning them for a year. Upon their release, the Magons fled to San Antonio, but, with Texas authorities working in tandem with Mexico, the brothers found themselves unwelcome there as well.

Using a $2,000 donation from wealthy Mexican landowner Francisco I. Madero, the Magons moved from San Antonio to St. Louis and restarted the publication of *Regeneracion* for their 30,000 subscribers. The paper was mailed from St. Louis to border towns in the Southwest, where it was smuggled into Mexico by railroad workers and others. Sometimes, it was hidden in hollowed-out Sears catalogs.

Through *Regeneracion*, the party called for secret groups to organize, plan a revolution, and send membership lists and money to St. Louis. Using St. Louis as their base, the brothers had between forty and seventy revolutionary cells around the United States and Mexico.

In St. Louis, the Magon brothers also founded El Partido Liberal Mexicano (Mexican Liberal Party) in September of 1905. The party called for better Mexican wages and working conditions, as well as an end to Diaz's dictatorship. However, U.S. officials, with substantial financial interests in Mexico, took a dim view of the "anarchists" in St. Louis. The brothers fled to Canada after being arrested in St. Louis for libel.

The Mexican Revolution gained steam in 1910; Porfirio Diaz resigned in 1911. Francisco Madero, the man who financed the Magons' move to St. Louis, was elected president.

Later, the Magon brothers were convicted for violating the U.S. neutrality laws and imprisoned at Leavenworth Penitentiary. Ricardo died in prison in 1922. A year later, Enrique was released and returned to Mexico, where he died in 1954.

Enrique and Ricardo Flores Magon, who fomented discontent and aroused workers, are considered influential thinkers who inspired and contributed to the Mexican Revolution. They did this, in part, from St. Louis. Today, streets, public schools, and towns in Mexico are named after the brothers.

Enrique Flores Magon. Courtesy Library of Congress

A St. Louisan Burns Atlanta and Shapes the Future of War

What would St. Louisans think today if one of their own burned homes, starved civilians, shot dogs, and purposely destroyed businesses and railroads? It's part of the legacy of William Tecumseh Sherman, a trolley executive turned general.

Sherman was president of the Fifth Street Railroad (a private streetcar company) at Broadway and Locust Street in St. Louis when violence at Fort Sumter instigated the Civil War in April 1861. He joined the Union Army and became a prominent general.

Sherman believed Southerners needed to pay a heavy price for splitting from the North, a treasonous action. And Sherman, more than other generals, believed the North had to target civilian morale and economic resources as much as the Confederate Army to win the war.

For example, he tore down Kentucky homes to repair a bridge the Confederate Army had destroyed. When

General William Sherman.
Courtesy Library of Congress

villagers asked for remuneration, he told them to bill the Confederacy. In Nashville, he refused local merchants space on trains for the transport of their goods. In Georgia, Sherman fed his 60,000 troops by taking food from farmers. "People may starve, and go without, but an army cannot and do its work," he said.

In his "March to the Sea," he burned Atlanta and destroyed "the roads which make Atlanta a place worth having." Sherman leveled farms and barns. He killed families' favorite dogs because they were used to track slaves. His goal was "to make Georgia howl."

Sherman continued through South Carolina and was determined to punish the state that had led secession.

Some historians attribute this concept of destroying non-military and civilian targets—called total war—to Sherman. Noted Princeton University Civil War historian James M. McPherson says Sherman's actions were "at least a step in the direction of total war because so many civilians suffered and some went hungry."

> Many are convinced this St. Louisan's tactics opened the way to the kind of warfare that culminated in World War II in places like London, Dresden, and Hiroshima.

In 1880, fifteen years after the end of the Civil War, Sherman said, "There is many a boy who looks on war as all glory, but, boys, it is all hell." The quotation has since been shortened to, "War is hell." The former St. Louis banker and streetcar executive's scorched earth policy was chronicled in the book and movie *Gone with the Wind.*

Jimmy Doolittle–Changed the Direction of the War in the Pacific

In April 1942, the United States needed an air crew to bomb Tokyo in retaliation for Japan's attack on Pearl Harbor four months earlier. There was only one problem: the American aircraft would only reach Tokyo and a little beyond, perhaps to China. The planes would not have enough fuel to safely complete a round-trip return to their carrier in the Pacific.

Any volunteers?

The call was answered by a St. Louis businessman, later described by the *New York Times* as "the first genuine American hero of World War II." He was Jimmy Doolittle, who grew up in Alaska and California and later studied aviation engineering. He received his doctorate in science from MIT. He became a record-setting test and stunt pilot in the 1920s.

Starting in 1930, Doolittle worked as an aviation manager and pilot for Shell Oil at 1221 Locust Street in downtown St. Louis. While here, Doolittle encouraged the United States to use 100-octane aviation gasoline in all Army aircraft. The idea was accepted and later paid major dividends to the country during wartime.

Doolittle, who lived at 6311 Washington Avenue, left Shell in 1940 for a year's service in the Army Air Corps. But Doolittle stayed put when the United States entered World War II a year later.

On April 18, 1942, Doolittle, who stood at five feet six inches and weighed 160 pounds, led the raid on Tokyo and four other Japanese cities. Doolittle's group of sixteen American B-25 bombers, each with a crew of five, took off from the *USS Hornet* aircraft carrier. Doolittle's Raiders, as they became known, bombed Tokyo, Yokohama, Kobe, Nagoya, and Osaka. While Doolittle and his crew bailed out over China and made their way to safety, all sixteen of the bombers were lost and eleven crew members were either captured or killed.

According to the *New York Times*, "One man was killed bailing out over China and two others drowned trying to swim a lake to escape capture by Japanese occupation forces. Of eight crewmen captured in China, three were executed. The remaining five were given life sentences, and one of them died of starvation."

Doolittle's Raiders lifted the morale of Americans at a time of otherwise discouraging war news from Europe and the Pacific. Doolittle's raid also showed the Japanese their country was vulnerable. As a result, Japan moved forces from the Pacific to its mainland to protect factories and shipyards. The shift allowed the United States to attain a strong position in Guadalcanal. In sum, the St. Louis businessman's raid changed the direction of the war in the Pacific.

President Roosevelt praised the crew, "With the apparent certainty of being forced to land in enemy territory or perish at sea, Colonel Doolittle personally led a squadron of Army bombers, manned by volunteer crews, in a highly destructive

Doolittle was the first pilot to fly blind in a completely covered cockpit. Unable to view the airspace or landscape, Doolittle flew his plane solely by instruments. This flight took place on September 29, 1929, on Long Island, New York.

Employees work on a B-25 bomber at an assembly plant in California. Doolittle and his raiders flew B-25s on the Tokyo bombing mission. Courtesy Library of Congress

raid on the Japanese mainland."

Doolittle later commanded thousands of planes in attacks on North Africa, Italy, and Germany.

> The Allied planes, using 100-octane aviation gasoline as Doolittle had recommended in St. Louis, flew longer and higher than enemy warplanes, a factor that played an important role in winning World War II.

After the war, Doolittle continued to work with Shell Oil until 1959 but not in St. Louis, as the company moved its Missouri operations to Houston and New York in the 1940s. Doolittle died in 1993.

The United States Was the First Nation to Recognize Israel ... Thanks to a St. Louisan

In May of 1948, the British withdrew troops from their Palestine protectorate. What was to become of the land? Jewish leaders implored President Harry Truman to recognize a country for Israel although Arab nations were threatening to destroy any new Jewish state. Proponents of Israel knew if the United States embraced Israel, so would its allies.

Secretary of State George Marshall, a leader in winning the war in Europe, advised the president to ignore Israel. He felt it would never be able to stand up to Arabs in the Middle East. However, Clark Clifford, Truman's White House counsel, disagreed. He felt Jews deserved their own country and the United States had an obligation to help the Jewish people after the atrocities of the Holocaust.

Truman, Clifford, and Marshall met to discuss Israel on May 12, 1948. Marshall exclaimed, "Mr. President, I don't even know why Clifford is here!" Marshall had a point. For when it came to international experience, Clifford was out of his league. Marshall had just led the United States to victory in Europe. Clifford, on the other hand, had no international or foreign policy experience whatsoever.

Clifford, who went to Soldan High School, worked as an attorney in St. Louis for Holland, Lashly and Donnell at 705 Olive Street from 1928 to 1943 before heading to Washington.

Historian Michael Beschloss recounts Truman was in awe of Marshall and his heroism in the war. So it must have been difficult when Marshall then yelled, "If you follow Clifford's advice and if I were to vote in the election, I would vote against you."

Truman was torn. On one hand, Clifford and Jewish leaders were imploring him to support a Jewish state. On the other, Marshall and the entire State Department feared such a move would infuriate Arabs, who would stop selling oil to the United States.

Clifford appealed to Truman's Baptist religion. He showed the president scriptural passages predicting the Jews "someday . . . would have their own homeland." Clifford also enlisted the help of Washington lawyer Max Lowenthal, who secretly prepared pro-Israel fact sheets and arguments for Clifford's use. Clifford warned Truman if he didn't support Israel, the Soviets would.

Two days later, just before midnight on May 14, 1948, David Ben-Gurion proclaimed the state of Israel in Tel Aviv. Within minutes, President Truman rejected the advice from the great general he admired and sided with the lawyer from St. Louis. Truman not only recognized the state of Israel but became the first world leader to do so.

Marshall never spoke to Clifford again.

What would have happened if Truman had not sought Clifford's advice? It's unknown. However, this we do know:

The United States aligned itself with Israel thanks to an attorney from St. Louis!

Larry Conners and *The Best Little Whorehouse in Texas*

How far will a reporter go to get a story?

In the case of Larry Conners, longtime anchor for KMOV, the answer is "all the way."

In 1973, Larry worked for KTRK-TV in Houston. His newsroom colleague Marvin Zindler was investigating the Chicken Ranch, a brothel operating near La Grange, Texas, for 123 years. Local and state authorities chose not to bust the operation for it was said the house had slept more politicians than the governor's mansion. A La Grange institution, its madam sponsored Little League teams and contributed to the local hospital foundation. Plus, the sheriff, of all people, pointed out the business resulted in no fights, low local rates of venereal disease, and no complaints.

"He makes that whore house sound like a damn nonprofit county recreational facility," Conners observed to *Texas Monthly* in 1973. Nonetheless, the brothel was illegal. And Zindler needed someone to actually use the establishment's services to prove its ill repute.

Twenty-five-year-old Conners, unmarried at the time, accepted the assignment. Posing as a college student on July 23, 1973, he went inside the brothel and hung around the parlor drinking a Coke and playing music on the jukebox. He secretly took a few photos.

As *Texas Monthly* described it, Larry's "inside work" discovered "first hand there really was prostitution going on in there."

Author Gary Taylor restated it another way, "Conners went undercover literally as a Chicken Ranch patron probing for proof that would provide the story with a hard foundation."

When the story by Zindler and Conners was broadcast and brought to the attention of Texas Governor Dolph Briscoe, the bordello was doomed. On August 1, 1973, the Chicken Ranch, the oldest continually operating non-floating whorehouse in the United States, closed down.

However, its reputation is now far from ill. ZZ Top wrote the song "La Grange" in honor of the establishment. Larry L. King turned the story into a Broadway musical and a movie *The Best Little Whorehouse in Texas*, starring Burt Reynolds and Dolly Parton.

In the movie, actor Charles Durning recites Conners' quote about the "damn nonprofit county recreational facility" almost verbatim.

The Walker and Davis Cups

Is St. Louis a great sports town? Certainly, and not just because of its pro sports teams. Two of sports' most prestigious competitions—the Walker Cup and the Davis Cup—were created by St. Louisans.

The Walker Cup is a trophy awarded on alternate years to the winner of an amateur golf tournament between the United States and Great Britain and Ireland. George Herbert Walker was the president of the U.S. Golf Association in 1920 when he invented the competition. Walker hoped to encourage golf on both sides of the Atlantic after World War I. He also donated the trophy. In the first Walker Cup match, a player for Great Britain fell ill and was replaced by Bernard Darwin, golf writer for the *Times of London*. Needless to say, that match had no trouble getting press coverage.

Walker grew up in St. Louis and attended school in England in the 1880s. He was the son of David Davis Walker, founder of Ely and Walker, the largest dry goods import firm west of the Mississippi. Together in 1904, the father and son built a summerhouse on what would be called Walker's Point in Kennebunkport, Maine.

By the 1920s, George Herbert Walker was on the boards of seventeen corporations and owned homes in Santa Barbara, Manhattan, South Carolina, and Long Island. His grandson and great grandson became presidents of the United States. (Gee, I thought "George Herbert Walker" rang a bell!)

Native St. Louisan Dwight Davis started the Davis Cup, an international tennis match. Davis, as a tennis player at Harvard College, organized a tennis competition between Great Britain and the United States. He planned the tournament, donated the trophy, and played for the United States in 1900, the Davis Cup's first year.

Those first matches were held at the Longwood Cricket Club in Chestnut Hill, Massachusetts (where your author worked as a bartender in 1981). By 1905, the tournament expanded to five nations. Today the Davis Cup is the world's largest annual team sports competition, with 130 countries represented annually.

Davis, when serving as St. Louis parks commissioner, opened up the first public tennis courts in the nation, yet another first for St. Louis! He later served as U.S. Secretary of War (now Defense), and governor-general of the Philippines.

Dwight Davis

Eads's Ironclad Ships Secure First Victories for the Union

Once in a while a human being will accomplish a feat of true astonishment. For example, in 1999, Fernando Tatis of the Cardinals hit his first two grand slams of his career. Not too remarkable until you consider: They both occurred on April 23 during the same inning against the same pitcher, Chan Ho Park of the Dodgers.

Amazing.

Achievements in the non-sports world aren't chronicled as much, but James Buchanan Eads racked up enough astounding accomplishments to fill an entire bookshelf.

First, at thirteen years old, he arrived in St. Louis on the steamboat *Carrollton*, which caught fire. Eight people perished in the blaze, but Eads jumped in the water and swam safely to shore.

Later, he made a fortune salvaging wrecks on the bottom of the Mississippi River. How? Eads invented a "diving bell"—an open-ended barrel attached to a hose for air—which he wore while walking on the river's sandy bottom. He also designed a railroad bridge at St. Louis even though he was not an engineer. One expert called his blueprints "entirely unsafe and impracticable." The structure, known as the Eads Bridge, has been in operation since 1874.

His greatest attainment came during the Civil War. Aligned with the North, Eads bid on a government contract to construct ironclad warships. Eads was concerned that if the Confederacy controlled the Mississippi River, then it might win the war.

The Navy had boats, but they got stuck in shallow water. Eads

Ironclad gunboats *St. Louis*, *Carondelet*, and *Cincinnati* at the Siege of Fort Henry. Courtesy Library of Congress

traveled to Washington with designs for gunboats that could sit in six feet of water. Although Navy experts were skeptical, Eads guaranteed he would build seven 500-ton ironclad gunboats within sixty-five days. The massive undertaking required the coordination of iron and steel supplies, labor, design, and management within an extremely tight window.

He signed a contract with the government on August 7, 1861. The task was gigantic because, in wartime, laborers were scattered, foundries and factories closed, and raw materials scarce. Nonetheless, Eads worked all available telegraph lines, secured 4,000 workers for the St. Louis shipyard in two weeks, built machines to manufacture his plates, and delivered his first gunboat by October 12, 1861. Eight boats were built within 100 days.

As the Union was short of funds, Eads ended up financing the ironclads with his own money. Eads' ships—he did indeed own them!—proved invaluable in February 1862 when they bombarded Forts Henry and Donelson. A Confederate soldier claimed their assault "exceeded in terror anything that the imagination had pictured . . . plowing roads through the earthworks and sandbags, dismantling guns . . . setting on fire and bringing down buildings within the fortification, and cutting in two, as with a scythe, large trees in the neighborhood."

With the help of this St. Louis businessman, the Union and General Ulysses Grant secured their first significant victories in the Civil War.

Quid Pro Quo: A St. Louis Favor Is Returned

By 1874, James Eads was about to open a bridge allowing, for the first time, trains to cross the Mississippi River at St. Louis. Steamboat owners opposed Eads, because, at the time, cargo and passengers could only cross the river by boat. And that's the way they liked it.

The ship owners convinced the Army Corps of Engineers to reject Eads's new bridge because some boats' smokestacks would be unable to fit under its arches in high water.

Hearings were held, but testimony was only solicited from boat owners. The Corps issued a report approving Eads's plans with one condition: he had to build a canal accommodating

James B. Eads. Courtesy Library of Congress

the few boats unable to pass under his new bridge. Otherwise, the entire project would have to be dismantled.

The cost of a canal would have been impossible. In fact, it probably would have been cheaper for Eads to purchase all of the boats unable to fit under his bridge!

Eads traveled to Washington and visited his old friend Ulysses Grant, now president of the United States. Grant owed Eads a favor dating back to his victories at Forts Henry and Donelson when Eads's ironclads made the difference in those battles.

Grant listened to Eads and then turned to Secretary of War William Belknap and said, "I think general, you had better drop the case."

Historian Howard S. Miller tells us, "The Corps of Engineers shelved the report."

The Eads Bridge opened on July 4, 1874.

Section Three

They Didn't Teach Me That in School

Toussaint L'Ouverture

Toussaint L'Ouverture was a Haitian slave-turned-revolutionary who put St. Louis on the U.S. map. L'Ouverture, who worked on a plantation in Haiti for more than four decades, led a revolution there against the British, Spanish, and French empires in the 1790s. French troops, arguably the best in the world at the time, failed miserably against the slave revolt.

The Haitian experience drained France's treasury. In need of money, Napoleon abandoned his plans to expand in North America and—to "surprised Americans"—offered to sell the entire Louisiana Territory, including St. Louis, to the United States for $15 million. Suddenly, St. Louis belonged to the United States thanks to this "Louisiana Purchase."

> St. Louis's Jefferson National Expansion Memorial, also known as the Gateway Arch, cost taxpayers $15 million, the same fee President Thomas Jefferson paid France for national expansion through "The Louisiana Purchase!"

What would have happened if the Haitian slave had not led a rebellion, depleted the French coffers, and forced the sale of France's North American real estate? Perhaps this book would be written in French.

Toussaint L'Ouverture. Courtesy Library of Congress

St. Louis: A French Village That Never Had a French Governor

Would somebody for the love of God please explain to me how the French village of St. Louis had Spanish governors and never one from France?

Read this slowly two or three times, because few cities have a history as convoluted as St. Louis.

Here goes: St. Louis was settled in 1764 by Pierre Laclede and Auguste Chouteau, representatives of the New Orleans–based Maxent, Laclede and Company, which had been granted a monopoly on fur trading in the area west of the Mississippi River near its confluence with the Missouri River. The fur traders—and apparently everyone else in New Orleans—were unaware until September 1764 that France had ceded the territory to the Spanish two years earlier. ("Now you tell me!")

That's one reason there was no French governor.

Next question: Why did Spain allow the French fur trappers to settle there?

Remember, Spain's rival Britain acquired what is now Illinois in the Treaty of Paris in 1763. In those days, Great "Where the Sun Never Sets" Britain wanted to rule the world. Literally.

Spain, seeking a buffer between British expansion and Spanish lands in Mexico, allowed the French to live in St. Louis with the most favorable conditions. For Spain in the eighteenth century, a French village at the confluence of the Mississippi and Missouri rivers was preferable to a village populated with Brits.

Later, in the 1780s, George Rogers Clark's Virginians made life difficult for the French Creoles in Illinois. As a result, the

Creoles fled to the relative safety of St. Louis, further populating St. Louis's French community.

By the 1790s, Spain was ready to sell Louisiana but not to the Americans. Spain feared the Yankees coveted their silver mines in Mexico. So, it secretly gave the Louisiana Territory to France on October 1, 1800, with the proviso Spain would have the offer of first refusal if France ever sold it. The deal also stipulated French soldiers would take the area as soon as they showed up.

They never did. And that's the second reason there was no French governor. One never showed up.

In 1803, Napoleon violated the agreement and sold St. Louis and the rest of the area to the United States in the Louisiana Purchase.

St. Louis: a French village that never had a French governor.

One City, One Day, Three Flags

On March 9, 1804, France officially transferred its land to the United States. It was time to remove the Spanish flag and replace it with Old Glory. In an attempt to soothe the wistful French villagers, authorities flew the French tri-color for twenty-four hours after the Spanish flag was lowered. Then, on March 10, the Stars and Stripes was raised.

It was likely the first and last time that one city for one day lived under the flags of three countries!

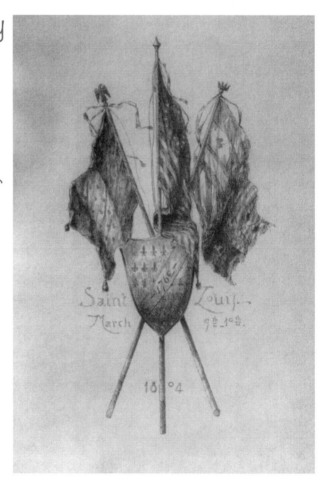

When Cuba Ruled St. Louis

Don't freak out, but it's a fact: Havana, at least on paper, used to control St. Louis!

Here's the deal: In 1762, France secretly ceded the Louisiana Territory to Spain in the Treaty of Fontainebleau.

In the 1763 Treaty of Paris, Spain got Havana from Great Britain. Spain then controlled its holdings in the New World through its outpost in Havana.

St. Louis was founded in February 1764. So, when the first Spanish lieutenant governor arrived in St. Louis in 1770, he reported to superiors in Havana.

If you haven't passed out yet due to shock, then make sure you sit down for this next bombshell: In 1787, St. Louis Roman Catholics were part of the diocese of Havana, Cuba.

Mark Twain Fought in the Civil War, But for Which Side?

In the Civil War, Missourians were divided between North and South. On whose side was young Samuel Clemens?

Because he wrote *Huckleberry Finn,* a novel attacking racism and showing the shared humanity of Huck and the slave Jim, it might be assumed Mark Twain joined the Northern army. What's more, Clemens had lived off and on in Union-dominated St. Louis since 1854.

Answer: A young Samuel Clemens never fought with the North. He spent several months in 1861 with a Confederate militia in northern Missouri.

Why just several months?

"I was incapacitated by fatigue through persistent retreating," he said.

Mark Twain. Courtesy Library of Congress

Jesuits Built SLU with Slaves

In 1823, a group of Jesuit priests moved from Maryland to Florissant, Missouri, bringing food, clothing, bibles, and—surprising but true—six slaves. Once here, the slaves washed clothes, cooked meals, and grew crops on the "priests' farm," officially named St. Stanislaus Jesuit Novitiate. Working most of their waking hours to benefit the priests, the "slaves had to take care of their own needs on their own time," according to historian C. Walker Gollar.

Fr. Charles Van Quickenborne, nicknamed "Napoleon" by the slaves, ordered whippings. Gollar tells us female slaves sometimes stepped in to prevent the floggings.

One Jesuit described the slaves as "without exception good people who complied with their Christian duties." The Jesuit slaves in St. Louis were baptized, confirmed, and married in the Roman Catholic tradition. They walked to St. Ferdinand Church in Florissant for Mass on Sundays.

In 1847, the superior of the United States Society of Jesus, Francis Dzierozynski, visited Florissant and ordered improvements to the slaves' inadequate quarters. He also granted approval for one slave to return to Maryland to visit his children—a directive Father Van Quickenborne ignored.

Jesuits were not the only Catholic leaders in St. Louis to own slaves. Mother Rose Philippine Duchesne of the Order of the Sacred Heart owned slaves. She was made a saint in the Roman Catholic Church in 1988.

St. Louis Bishops William Dubourg and Joseph Rosati also owned slaves. In fact, slaves seeking freedom filed suits against Bishop Rosati in 1837 and 1840. According to court records, Rosati appears to have prevailed in both cases.

St. Stanislaus Seminary in Florissant, 1847. Courtesy Library of Congress

Dzierozynski instructed the St. Louis Jesuits to only sell their slaves with his permission and then only "to humane and Christian masters" who would purchase them for their own use. Gollar writes that two years later Van Quickenborne, who had not yet improved the slaves' quarters, sold a seven-year-old slave named Peter. Father Peter John De Smet wrote, "His poor parents . . . constantly lament his loss." Dzierozynski later intervened, and Peter was returned to his parents. By this point, Van Quickenborne was despised by slaves and fellow Jesuits alike.

Using proceeds from the farm, the Jesuits opened their college on Washington Avenue between Ninth and Tenth streets on November 2, 1829. A slave served as cook. This school would later become known as Saint Louis University.

To put the St. Louis priests' slave-holding in context, Roman Catholic leaders in Europe at the time called slavery "violent and barbaric." Non-religious entities, like the state of Vermont in 1777, had already prohibited slavery.

The St. Louis Jesuits owned about twenty slaves in the 1830s. Their slaves dwindled to a few by 1865 when Missouri slaves were emancipated. The Jesuits built St. Elizabeth's Church in 1873 for African-American Catholics in St. Louis.

The Grants Had Slaves...
During the Civil War!

Truth, as they say, is stranger than fiction. How else to explain one of U.S. history's great ironies: While Union General Ulysses S. Grant was winning the war that abolished slavery in the United States, his family owned slaves.

Before the war, Grant lived on a farm in St. Louis from 1854 to 1859. His family's slaves cleaned, cooked, kept the fires going, served as nurses, etc. In 1859, Ulysses Grant emancipated the one slave he personally owned at the Old Courthouse in downtown St. Louis.

A year later, the family planned a move from St. Louis to Galena, Illinois. Missouri allowed slavery; Illinois did not. The Grants still had four family slaves given to them by Mrs. Grant's father. If taken to Illinois, they would be free. Instead of freeing them, the Grants hired out their slaves to masters in Missouri before moving to Galena.

War broke out in April 1861, and Grant eventually became the commanding general for the Union. On January 1, 1863, President Lincoln's Emancipation Proclamation freed slaves in Rebel-held territory. Lincoln's generals retained their slaves. After the capture of Vicksburg in July 1863, Julia Dent Grant and her children visited General Grant at his headquarters. According to historian H. W. Brands, "Confederate women in Mississippi . . . observed that she was accompanied by one of the Dent family's slaves."

Yes, even after the Emancipation Proclamation, General Grant's family continued to use slaves for labor. All Missouri slaves were freed by the state's constitutional convention in January 1865.

Forest Park Honors Both Sides of One War

During the Civil War, St. Louis was truly divided. The city was the hub of a slaveholding state fighting for the Union's preservation. This contradiction is reflected in the monuments of the signature Forest Park.

Since St. Louis was officially part of the North, it's no surprise Forest Park honors Union leaders with statues of President Abraham Lincoln's attorney general, Edward Bates; the organizer of the first volunteer Union army in the South, Francis Preston Blair Jr.; and Union General Franz Sigel.

Here's where it gets interesting: Forest Park is also home to a Confederate memorial.

In 1912, the Ladies Confederate Monument Association sought proposals for a statue in Forest Park, so long as it contained "no figure of a Confederate soldier or object of modern warfare."

Though the Confederate monument was proposed almost fifty years after the Civil War's end, it sparked local debate. Some did not want to honor soldiers from the South. Others were afraid St. Louis would lose business in the South if it prohibited the memorial.

Even the sculptors in the design competition were at each others' throats. Frederick Ruckstuhl charged George Zolnay's entry—portraying a young man surrounded by worried loved ones as he prepared to leave for war—a violation of the competition's rules prohibiting any display of Confederate soldiers.

Zolnay shot back. He called Ruckstuhl "a pest" and claimed

Ruckstuhl's design was "suitable for a wedding cake." Ruckstuhl then called Zolnay "grotesque."

However grotesque, Zolnay won the competition.

The St. Louis Board of Aldermen passed an ordinance approving the memorial, an action never needed for other park monuments.

The Confederate memorial was unveiled on December 15, 1914. The inscription reads in part, "Erected in memory of soldiers and sailors of the Confederate States . . . who fought to uphold the right declared by the pen of Jefferson and achieved by the sword of Washington. . . . History contains no chronicle more illustrious than the story of their achievements. . . ."

Thus, a park in St. Louis showcases memorials to both sides of one war. How many cities in the world can make the same claim?

The American Revolution Hits St. Louis

Quick: think of a Revolutionary War battlefield. Valley Forge. Concord. Lexington. Bunker Hill. St. Louis.

St. Louis?

In May of 1780, British soldiers and their Indian allies camped a few miles from what is now downtown St. Louis. At the time, St. Louis was a small sixteen-year-old village controlled by Spain but populated with French fur traders. Spain was quietly aiding the American Revolution to Great Britain's annoyance.

Concerned about a possible attack, the Spanish governor built a stone tower thirty feet in diameter and thirty-five feet tall. He called it Fort San Carlos. The fort was largely built with funds and labor donated by St. Louis settlers.

The local militia included "eighty-five boatmen, forty-six farmers, thirty-eight merchants and traders, twenty-four hunters, twenty-three artisans, one constable and one musician." Good thing they had the musician!

On May 26, 1780, about 1,200 redcoats and Indians attacked Fort San Carlos. They were met with cannon fire from the tower and blazing muskets from the trenches.

The Indians captured a few villagers outside the fort and disemboweled them, an action intended to draw angry townspeople out of the fort. The locals did not take the bait.

Although far outnumbered, the St. Louis villagers prevailed over the most powerful army on the planet! The St. Louisans' victory at the Battle of Fort San Carlos prevented the British from gaining a stronghold in the Mississippi Valley.

POWs in St. Louis

The 1960s sitcom *Hogan's Heroes* portrayed the comedic life inside a German POW camp. Is it possible the TV show was based on a true story but one where the POWs were Germans and Italians?

During World War II, as Americans fought the Axis powers in Europe, the U.S. government sent hundreds of German and Italian prisoners of war to the St. Louis area. While here, the POWs drank in bars, drove trucks, enjoyed midnight trysts, and even worked in a St. Louis munitions plant. As author David Fiedler relates in *The Enemy Among Us: POWs in Missouri During World War II*, they redefined the word "prisoner."

Many of the POWs stayed in barracks at the family-owned Hellwig Brothers Farm in Chesterfield's Gumbo Flats area, which offered a swimming pool, recorded and live music, art supplies, books, musical instruments, and Ping-Pong.

On Sundays, Italian POWs primarily attended Ascension Roman Catholic Church in Chesterfield, but some attended Mass at St. Ambrose Church on the Hill, St. Louis's largely Italian neighborhood. They also ate dinner in the community's homes and restaurants. All exits were guarded by military police. Italian POWs also made trips to the Fox Theatre to watch movies.

In April 1944, Italian POWs were moved elsewhere in Missouri and replaced by German prisoners of war who were remembered as less friendly than the Italians. The Catholic Germans did not go to confession or receive Holy Communion, although they did attend Mass. Fiedler tells us the German POWs who fraternized with Americans got their knuckles broken by fellow Germans in the camp.

Due to a wartime labor shortage in St. Louis, POWs were put to work. They cut trees, removed brush, and harvested corn. Some POWs—living on a houseboat—repaired levees on the Missouri River. One of these floating camps was based on the Mississippi River at Arsenal Street and another in the Baden neighborhood near Humboldt and Broadway.

German POWs also worked in the private sector, performing nursery work and construction in Kirkwood, Des Peres, Sappington, and Produce Row in St. Louis. Curiously, some POWs were allowed to drive trucks. Others were put to work at the St. Louis Ordnance Depot, which manufactured and repaired munitions. (It is hard to imagine enemy combatants from, say, Al Qaeda performing the same work in the twenty-first century.)

In October 1945, two Germans escaped Chesterfield in a heavy downpour. According to Fiedler, they headed for South America and got all the way to Waterloo, Illinois, before

Japanese Internees

Before POWs arrived in St. Louis, authorities used the Hellwigs' Chesterfield farm to house Japanese-Americans suspected of having questionable wartime allegiances.

One day in 1942, Verna Hellwig drove to St. Louis to pick up a Japanese-American family at Union Station. On the trip back to Chesterfield, Hellwig's truck got a flat tire. According to Fiedler, a Japanese-American detainee walked to a filling station, borrowed a jack, and fixed Ms. Hellwig's tire.

The Japanese internees in Chesterfield moved out in 1944 to make way for Italian prisoners of war.

succumbing to cold and hunger. The two posed as hitchhikers on Route 3 in Illinois, got in a car, and asked the driver to take them back to Chesterfield.

A prisoner of war's life in St. Louis was not all work. In one case, an Italian POW borrowed a little girl's bike on the Hellwig farm for a romantic rendezvous outside the camp. Fiedler reports some German POWs drank beers at the Countryside Inn on Schoettler Road between Conway and Olive. No guard was with them.

The war ended in 1945. All POWs were discharged from St. Louis by March 31, 1946. The St. Louis POW story did not entirely end there. Remember the two Germans who tried to escape and were escorted back to Chesterfield?

They exchanged Christmas cards with their Illinois driver until 1977!

Why Roswell Field Moved to St. Louis

Dred Scott's suit for freedom was the most famous court case in U.S. history. Yet his attorney, Roswell Field, was a newcomer to St. Louis from Vermont, where he had never studied or practiced slave law. After all, Vermont had no slaves. So, how did Dred Scott connect with Roswell Field?

Here's the story, one of the strangest in St. Louis legal history:

Roswell Field was born in 1807 in Vermont, which abolished slavery in its constitution in 1777. Field graduated from Middlebury College in 1822 at age fifteen. By then, he was proficient in six languages: Greek, Latin, Spanish, German, French, and English, of course. In 1825, at age eighteen, Field was admitted to the Vermont bar.

In 1832, he married eighteen-year-old Mary Elmira Phelps in Putney, Vermont. However, Ms. Phelps had been engaged to Jeremiah Clark of Boston prior to the wedding and her mother had a fit when she learned of the marriage. At the insistence of her mother and brothers, Mary Phelps wrote Field a letter saying she was engaged to another man and was tricked into marriage by Field. Furthermore, she insisted, "I therefore write this to inform you I am not willing on any account to see you again."

Phelps proceeded to marry Clark, became pregnant, and moved with him to Boston.

Field sued, insisting his marriage certificate was a legal and binding contract. The case dragged on for seven years. Phelps testified the marriage was obtained "by the force, violence, frauds and circumvention of the said Field" and "it was her wish the ceremony was to be considered a nullity."

On July 2, 1839, a chancery court ruled in favor of Mary Elmira Phelps, by then a widow. The defeat was hard on Field personally and publicly, since he had been a lawyer of some standing as well as a member of Vermont's General Assembly.

Immediately after losing in court, a humiliated Roswell Field escaped his embarrassment in Vermont and moved to St. Louis, where he started a legal practice that included slave law. Later, working for free, Roswell Field guided Dred Scott's case all the way to the Supreme Court of the United States. Scott lost in a landmark, nation-splitting decision that led to the election of Abraham Lincoln and the onset of the Civil War.

What if Mary Phelps had not dumped Roswell Field? It is doubtful he would have moved west. Would Dred Scott have found another St. Louis lawyer to take his case pro bono? Would there have been a Dred Scott case? A President Lincoln?

The Mystery of Lloyd Gaines

One of St. Louis's best and brightest burst like a shooting star onto the national scene in the 1930s. And, also like a meteor, he disappeared just as quickly.

In 1931, Lloyd Gaines graduated first in his class at St. Louis's Vashon High School and later got his bachelor's degree at all-black Lincoln University, where he was president of his senior class and an honors history graduate. Gaines decided he wanted to be an attorney, although Missouri in 1936 had few African-American lawyers, perhaps three dozen or so.

When Gaines applied for admission to the all-white University of Missouri Law School, he became the first black man to do so. His application was rejected. The school told him if he were to apply and get accepted to an out-of-state law school, Missouri would pay his tuition.

Gaines sued and lost his case in state court. He appealed and, while earning a master's degree in economics at the University of Michigan, took his case all the way to the U.S. Supreme Court.

On December 12, 1938, Gaines won his case in a 6-2 Supreme Court decision (a vacancy existed on the nine-judge panel).

It was the beginning of the end for segregated schools in Missouri and elsewhere. The *New York Times* called the decision a legal "steppingstone toward Brown v. Board of Education, the landmark 1954 decision that repudiated the 'separate but equal' notion in outlawing school segregation."

But four months later in the evening of March 19, 1939, Lloyd Gaines, twenty-eight, left an apartment in Chicago to buy some postage stamps. He was never seen again. His family never filed a missing-person report.

The University of Missouri granted a posthumous honorary doctor of law degree to Gaines in 2006.

> Those who are wise will shine as bright as the sky, and those who lead many to righteousness will shine like the stars forever.
> —Daniel 12:3

St. Louis's Communist Auditor

Joseph Weydemeyer was a friend of Karl Marx and a one-time member of the German Communist League before fleeing to the United States in 1848. After working in New York and then serving in the Union Army during the Civil War, Weydemeyer served as St. Louis County auditor in the 1860s.

And you thought today's politicians were liberal!

The Lie That Snagged the Republican National Convention

My favorite line about St. Louis summers belongs to David Francis, still the only person to serve as both mayor of St. Louis and governor of Missouri. Francis also organized the 1904 World's Fair.

In 1895, he traveled to New York to lure the 1896 GOP National Convention to St. Louis. According to biographer Harper Barnes, Francis was asked by a *New York Times* reporter, "Is it not likely to be very warm in St. Louis?"

Francis outrageously claimed, "No. It would not be so uncomfortably warm as it would be here in New York. The atmosphere is not so humid in St. Louis as it is in New York. When the thermometer stands at 90 degrees here, it is more uncomfortable than it is in St. Louis when the temperature is 110 degrees."

The next summer, the Republicans, without air conditioning, nominated William McKinley in St. Louis.

Yes, Francis was a Democrat.

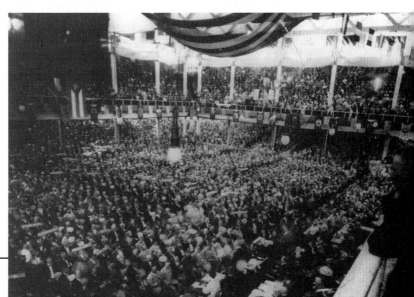

The 1896 GOP National Convention in St. Louis. Courtesy Library of Congress

If the School Was Chartered on February 2, Would It Now Be "Groundhog U?"

February 22 is the birthday of one of our most enduring institutions. On this date in 1853 Missouri State Senator Wayman Crow introduced a bill chartering a school of higher learning in St. Louis. Governor Sterling Price signed the measure into law. All of this was done on February 22 because the new school would be named after George Washington, right?

Not exactly.

The new school was named Eliot Seminary. Crow wanted the school named after his friend William Greenleaf Eliot Jr., the Unitarian minister and educator. On that day, Eliot wrote in his journal, "An 'Eliot Seminary' has been incorporated by (the) legislature, but I know nothing of it."

Eliot wanted a new school of higher learning but not one with his name on it. He favored academic independence and feared, because of his religious profession, an institute named in his honor would be considered sectarian.

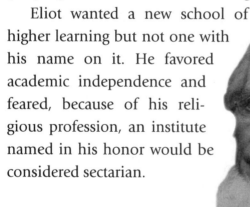

William Greenleaf Eliot.
Courtesy Library of
Congress

Members of the new school's board met on February 22, 1854, the first anniversary of the school's charter. Eliot announced the school would be named Washington Institute because it had received its charter, *by coincidence*, on George Washington's birthday.

Perhaps if the school's charter had been adopted on April 13 we would have a Thomas Jefferson University in St. Louis. Or, if the charter incorporation happened on October 30, the school would be known as John Adams University.

Officially, Washington University became its name in 1857.

St. Louis: The City Founded by an Eighth Grader!

St. Louis has many distinctions, but the most overlooked, in this author's opinion, is the age of its founder.

In February 1764, Auguste Chouteau led thirty men to clear trees and build cabins for what is now St. Louis.

Chouteau was born on September 7, 1749. You can do the math. He was fourteen at the time.

Fourteen!

At fourteen, in today's St. Louis, Chouteau would not be old enough to drive, work, smoke, vote, join the military, or drink a beer. Yet this young teenager was able to "supervise the initial construction" of a great American city.

Chouteau was clerk to his mother's boyfriend Pierre Laclede, who picked out the location for St. Louis in 1763 and sent Chouteau to establish a fur trading post after the winter's thaw. Laclede did not visit the settlement until April 1764.

So, St. Louis's founding father was more like a founding boy.

Let's face it, aside from Mozart who composed music at age five, has any other human being accomplished as much as Auguste Chouteau at such a young age?

St. Louis Can't Agree On a Founding Date

St. Louis was founded in 1764. But on what date in 1764 was the city founded?

Surprisingly, that is a difficult question.

Historian Charles van Ravenswaay, director of the Missouri Historical Society from 1946 to 1962, wrote that fur trader Pierre Laclede "sent young (Auguste) Chouteau with thirty men to clear the site. They arrived late in the afternoon of February 14 . . ."

Historian James Neal Primm concurred. He wrote, "On February 14, 1764, a working party of thirty employees of Maxent, Laclede and Company of New Orleans, headed by Auguste Chouteau, an extraordinary young man of fourteen years, stepped ashore from a bateau to the west bank of the Mississippi River . . ."

However, historian Frederick Fausz believes the only eyewitness to document the founding was Chouteau, and his original manuscript notes the founding on February 15, with an "oddly shaped numeral '5.'" Fausz insists the February 15 founding is supported by "conclusive and well-publicized visual evidence," whereas supporters of the February 14 theory, Fausz believes, rely on "flawed secondary sources."

Greg Ames, a curator at the Mercantile Library, agrees with Fausz. He told Tim O'Neil of the *St. Louis Post-Dispatch* in 2010: "We have many interesting questions about that (Chouteau's) manuscript, but the number 5 isn't one of them."

Fausz bolsters his argument by noting the city's first public celebration of its birthday was on February 15, 1847, "even though it fell on a less-than-convenient Monday for large parades, banquets and balls."

It's hard to believe a city can't quite agree on when it was founded. Alas, blame it on poor penmanship. But, of this, there can be no debate: arguing about St. Louis began on day one. Whenever that was.

Section Four

Strange St. Louis Pairings

Dream Team Roommates

William Clark owned property in 1838 at 101-103 Main Street, where the north leg of the Gateway Arch stands today. Clark, who traveled with Meriwether Lewis to the Pacific Ocean and back between 1804 and 1806, also served as governor of the Missouri Territory and superintendent of Indian Affairs. He was also a successful fur trader.

Clark's buildings on this property included his home—a large two-story house built in 1816—as well as a small two-man cottage and a 300-square-foot brick building. In May of 1838, Clark rented the brick building to Dr. William Beaumont, a U.S. military surgeon, known to this day as one of medical science's leading researchers of gastric physiology and the human digestive system. Beaumont Hospital in Michigan, Beaumont High School in St. Louis, and Beaumont Army Medical Center in Texas are named in his honor.

At the same time, Clark rented his cottage to Robert E. Lee, an army lieutenant working in St. Louis to fix structural problems in the St. Louis harbor. Later, Lee would famously command the South's military against the North in the Civil War.

Facing page: William Clark. Above left, Dr. William Beaumont. Above right: General Robert E. Lee. Courtesy Library of Congress

Thus, for at least one month, three historic figures—Clark, Lee, and Beaumont—known around the world for tremendous accomplishments in their respective fields—exploration, military, and medicine—lived together on the same piece of property in downtown St. Louis!

Two Favorite Sons in the Same Presidential Election

St. Louisans had a political dilemma in 1868. They had to choose between two men with local ties running against each other in the presidential election. Ulysses S. Grant was nominated for president by the Republican Party, and Francis Blair ran for vice president on the Democratic side.

Grant had married Julia Dent, a St. Louisan, and tried his best as a farmer here in the 1850s.

Blair was a St. Louis attorney and a Union hero in the North's efforts to control St. Louis. After the war, Blair switched parties and in 1868 sought his party's presidential nomination but lost it to New York Governor Horatio Seymour. Blair became Seymour's running mate.

Grant won the election. In Missouri, he got 57 percent of the vote.

Francis Blair (left) and Ulysses Grant. Courtesy Library of Congress

The St. Louis Connection That Secured the Surrender

On July 3, 1863, at the Civil War's Battle of Vicksburg, Confederate General John Pemberton prepared to surrender to Ulysses S. Grant. Pemberton sent an emissary, General John Bowen, with a white flag to Grant's camp. Bowen's role was to convey Pemberton's intentions and discover Grant's terms for surrender.

Grant told Bowen any surrender would be unconditional.

Grant repeated his terms the next day when he met with both Bowen and Pemberton. An upset Pemberton abruptly turned to leave the meeting.

The bloody Vicksburg battle probably would have resumed immediately if not for Bowen, who suddenly jumped up and asked for a private conversation with one of Grant's officers. Perhaps, Bowen hoped, they could work out a compromise. Grant, without promising to be bound by any discussions, agreed to allow the meeting.

After conferencing with General A. J. Smith, Bowen proposed all Confederate soldiers at Vicksburg be allowed to keep their weapons once they surrendered. Bowen's suggestion was rejected by Grant, but it seemed to trigger something in his thinking.

That evening, Grant wrote Pemberton a letter with new terms. Grant relaxed his rules a bit. He would allow surrendering Confederate officers to keep their sidearms and horses, and would release—not capture—rebel soldiers.

Why did Grant accommodate Bowen's requests and relax

the terms of surrender? Why did Union General Ulysses Grant pay any heed to Confederate General John Bowen? Perhaps because Grant, as he later wrote in his memoirs, knew Bowen well and thought "favorably" of him—the two had been St. Louis neighbors in the late 1850s!

Longstreet, Grant's Best Man?

On April 8, 1865, Confederate General Robert E. Lee decided to surrender his forces to end the Civil War. Lee sent two generals, James "Pete" Longstreet and John Gordon, with a note expressing his intentions to Union General Ulysses S. Grant's camp near Appomattox, Virginia.

After Lee's official, historic surrender the next day at the McLean farm, Grant met with several of the Confederate generals, including Longstreet. Grant took Longstreet's arm and said, "Pete, let's have another game of brag (cards) to recall the old days." Grant gave him a cigar. Longstreet recalled it was "gratefully received."

For some in the Union Army, General Longstreet was the fierce adversary they faced at Second Bull Run, Fredericksburg, Antietam, and Gettysburg. However, for Grant, Longstreet was more than just a battlefield foe. The two had attended West Point together. Longstreet was also the cousin of Grant's wife, Julia. What's more, Longstreet, the man whose forces aimed to annihilate Grant's, served as best man at Grant's 1848 wedding in St. Louis!

Grant and Longstreet had been enemies and friends. Perhaps that's one reason Grant wrote such generous terms of surrender at Appomattox, allowing Lee's soldiers to keep their side arms and horses, and sending his commissary to feed the hungry Confederate soldiers.

Clark Clifford and William McChesney Martin Jr.

Was there ever a more powerful lineup than the 1922 tennis team at Soldan High School in St. Louis?

William McChesney Martin Jr. was called "the boy wonder of Wall Street" when, at thirty-one, he became the first paid president of the New York Stock Exchange. He left his $48,000-a-year job at the exchange to serve in World War II where he earned twenty-one dollars a month. As chairman of the Federal Reserve Board for nineteen years (1951–1970) from Presidents Harry Truman to Richard Nixon, Martin presided over what was then the longest period of economic expansion in the nation's history.

Clark Clifford was one of the most connected Democrats in the second half of the twentieth century. Starting as White House counsel to President Truman, he urged the United States to recognize the nation of Israel. He worked to downplay Ted Kennedy's expulsion from Harvard for cheating, and he later defended John F. Kennedy over allegations his Pulitzer Prize–winning book *Profiles in Courage* was ghostwritten. As Secretary of Defense, he told President Lyndon Johnson the Vietnam War was a losing battle.

Clifford and Martin were doubles partners on the Soldan High School tennis team in 1922.

The "St. Louis Blues" and W. C. Handy

For two weeks in 1893, a hungry and unshaven homeless musician named W. C. Handy slept on cobblestones underneath the Eads Bridge in St. Louis. He spotted a woman on the riverfront who seemed to be in even worse shape. She cried that her man had "a heart like a rock."

These words became part of Handy's popular 1914 composition, "St. Louis Blues." It was nearly the most-recorded song of the first half of the twentieth century, second only to "Silent Night."

Handy was not always homeless. Around 1900, he lived and played music on Targee Street in a neighborhood called Chestnut Valley. Today, the Scottrade Center is where Targee Street used to be. And what NHL team plays hockey inside the Scottrade Center? In an amazing coincidence, that team would be the St. Louis Blues.

W. C. Handy in 1941. Courtesy Library of Congress

The Strange Fate of Joseph E. Johnston

William Tecumseh Sherman lived on and off in St. Louis before and after the Civil War, where he distinguished himself as one of the leading generals for the Union. Secessionist General Joseph E. Johnston fought and lost to Sherman's army in Atlanta in 1864. On April 26, 1865, Johnston surrendered the Army of Tennessee as well as all active Confederate forces in the Carolinas, Florida, and Georgia to Sherman.

So the two were bitter enemies, right?

Actually, after the war, Johnston became friends with Sherman. In fact, he served as a pallbearer at Sherman's funeral on February 19, 1891, in New York. Out of respect for Sherman, the eighty-two-year-old Johnston refused to wear a hat despite the day's icy rain. When others in the funeral party encouraged him to cover his head, Johnston replied, "If I were in his place and he standing here in mine, he would not put on his hat."

As a result, Johnston contracted pneumonia and died a month later on March 21, 1891.

A second funeral procession concluding with Sherman's burial at Calvary Cemetery took place in St. Louis two days later on February 21, 1891.

How St. Louis *Almost* Became Disney World

Is there a St. Louis connection to Disney? Well, let's just say it's a small world after all. Here's the story:

In 1963, St. Louis leaders invited Missouri native Walt Disney to create a movie commemorating the city's 200th birthday in 1964. But Disney countered with his own blockbuster idea—a new Disney attraction in St. Louis to complement the upcoming Gateway Arch and Busch Stadium projects. Called Riverfront Square, it would be on two city blocks bound by Broadway, Market, Walnut, and Seventh streets.

In April 1963, Disney executive Donn Tatum, and Harrison "Buzz" Price of the Economic Research Associates, a Disneyland consultant, visited key St. Louis businessmen. A month later, Disney himself visited St. Louis with his wife, Lillian, and daughter Sharon. The Disneys toured the Gateway Arch and Busch Stadium, both under construction.

Historian Dan Viets tells us Disney was impressed with downtown St. Louis's highway intersections. "It's great to see a city that has recognized its needs and is doing something about it," Disney said. However, Disney was concerned how many people would visit Riverfront Square in the winter. In August 1963, Buzz Price released a report showing Riverfront Square could be profitable.

Disney visited St. Louis again in November and suggested exhibits highlighting Jefferson, Napoleon, Twain, and St. Louis. Disney said the new venture, ". . . would make parts of Disneyland obsolete." Some in St. Louis feared Disney's

What was Disney's vision for St. Louis? His ideas included a town square, a Lewis and Clark Adventure ride, an old St. Louis section, and an old New Orleans section. Visitors would also experience a Caribbean Pirate's Lair, a "Haunted House," and both a Blue Bayou boat ride and a Western Riverboat Ride. According to historian Dan Viets, the plans were drawn by Marvin Aubrey Davis, who later designed Disney World. Patrons would also experience restaurants, shops, concessions, banquet facilities, two 360-degree Circarama theaters, a Meramec Cave ride, an "Old Opera House Theater," and other rides based on Disney cartoons.

project would clash with local architecture. Of greater concern, at least to Anheuser-Busch President August Busch Jr., was Disney's demand that no alcohol be served at the attraction. According to retired Admiral Joe Fowler, the first general manager of Disneyland, Busch said, "Any man who would build something like this, and then not serve beer and liquor inside, is crazy!" The remark was made at a private gathering in St. Louis with Disney within earshot. Fowler believed it doomed the St. Louis project.

Two days later, Preston Estep, chairman of the Civic Center Redevelopment Corporation, said, "Any plans developed by Mr. Disney or anyone else would not be approved if they did not make provisions for the sale of beer, wine and liquor in the restaurant and other appropriate entertainment facilities in the area. . . ."

St. Louisans feared the worst: They would lose Disney's new project. The *St. Louis Globe-Democrat* editorial page asked,

"Can't Mr. Disney realize on his part that a Sahara in downtown St. Louis would be somewhat out of character?"

Despite differences, Disney drew up plans for a St. Louis project in January and February of 1964. He planned on renaming the project, keeping it in a single building with five levels, and serving alcoholic beverages in "adults only" sections, as was done in "dry" Disneyland where visitors seeking to imbibe could take a monorail to a nearby hotel.

However, Disney and local leaders could not agree on the project's funding. Disney wanted to own the project, and he wanted the city to finance it. On July 13, 1965, both parties announced the project was dead.

In November 1965, Disney announced publicly for the first time he was planning a new major attraction in Orlando, Florida.

How the U.N. *Almost* Came to Weldon Spring

After the United Nations was established on June 26, 1945, world leaders needed to find a site for the organization's new headquarters. The St. Louis Chamber of Commerce volunteered a former ordnance plant in Weldon Spring. Perhaps oblivious to the irony—or was it poetry?—of locating a peace organization where TNT used to be produced, Missouri Governor Phil Donnelly and St. Louis Mayor Aloys Kaufmann also supported the plan.

The St. Louis effort pointed to the centrality of the region; it was in the middle of the country and roughly equidistant from Asia and Europe. Former Secretary of State Edward R. Stettinius wanted the UN to be in the center of the United States and also endorsed Weldon Spring.

Believe it or not, other Missouri cities were proffered. Governor Donnelly also proposed consideration of Jefferson City to a UN delegate. The president of the University of Kansas City recommended his city to Harry Truman when he awarded him an honorary degree in June 1945. And C. H. Spink of Fort Worth, Texas, suggested the Lake of the Ozarks.

How close did we actually get to landing all those international ambassadors of the United Nations, the world's largest, foremost, and most prominent international organization? The St. Louis delegation traveled to London to make its case. Despite the benefits of Weldon Spring, the United Nations voted to locate in New York City.

Alton Was Considered a Site for the Air Force Academy

In 1949, U.S. Air Force Secretary Stuart Symington appointed a board to find a site for the nation's new Air Force Academy. Symington, a former CEO of Emerson Electric in St. Louis, preferred Alton, Illinois, and the river town immediately became a frontrunner among cities seeking to serve as home to the military school.

After 600 locations were considered, it came down to Alton and Colorado Springs, Colorado. That's when Colorado played dirty.

Colorado Springs Ford dealer R. Soland Doenges, head of his city's chamber of commerce, paid a visit to Alton. Wearing a fake beard, sunglasses, and old clothes, he stirred up local opposition to the project. He badmouthed the Air Force and encouraged the locals to treat the Air Force and its selection board with disdain. He even gave newspaper interviews posing as an Alton-area resident upset with the prospect of hosting the new academy.

Meanwhile, in Colorado Springs, Doenges and others rolled out the red carpet for the selection board. They made sure board members stayed at the best hotels and were welcomed by banners on buildings. Colorado also promised to provide land for the Air Force and build any necessary expressways.

The Colorado backers asked Charles Lindbergh if he would scan their proposed location by air. When the famed pilot arrived in the Colorado Springs airport to rent a plane, the crusty airport manager asked him if he knew how to fly. Lindbergh said, "I think I can fly."

The skeptical manager asked Lindbergh if he had a pilot's license. Lindbergh pulled out a dozen licenses from all over the world and laid them on the gentleman's desk. The manager asked, "You ain't Charles Lindbergh, be you?"

Although Lindbergh favored Alton, after his flyover he concluded Colorado Springs was a suitable location.

Meanwhile, Christian Scientists started a letter-writing campaign urging leaders to spare Principia College from any development by the Air Force.

While Symington personally favored Alton, he made no attempt to influence the committee. By the time the decision was made, Symington was in the U.S. Senate.

On June 24, 1954, Air Force Secretary Harold E. Talbot announced the decision: The new facility would go to Colorado Springs. For Coloradans, it was the best day since Zebulon Pike discovered Pikes Peak.

Since Colorado Springs became home to the Air Force Academy, its population has risen from 45,000 to 426,000.

Elizabeth Keckley and Mary Todd Lincoln

If Elizabeth Keckley's life story was presented as fiction, readers would say it was too outlandish.

Keckley was a slave in St. Louis who designed dresses for the city's wealthiest and most fashionable women. In 1855, with the help of Mrs. Elizabeth LeBourgeois, Keckley raised $1,200 to purchase freedom for herself and her son. Keckley stayed in St. Louis making dresses until she generated enough income to repay her benefactors. In 1860, she moved to Washington, D.C.

In the nation's capital, Keckley continued to make dresses and immediately acquired a "who's who" clientele of Washington: Mrs. Jefferson Davis, Mrs. Robert E. Lee, and Mrs. Abraham

Elizabeth Keckley (left) and Mary Todd Lincoln. Courtesy Library of Congress

Lincoln. Keckley made about fifteen dresses for the First Lady.

Keckley became close friends with Mary Todd Lincoln. The two were probably closer than any First Lady and a black woman at that time in the nation's history. Tragedies tightened their friendship. Keckley lost her son, George, in the Civil War in 1861. Lincoln lost her eleven-year-old son Willie to typhoid fever in 1862. They consoled each other.

When President Lincoln was shot and killed, Mrs. Lincoln called for Keckley, her "best living friend."

Keckley's incredible story defied all odds—freed slaves did not travel in elite circles, much less inside the White House. It would not last.

Keckley published a tell-all memoir, *Behind the Scenes; or, Thirty Years a Slave and Four Years in the White House.* Lincoln felt betrayed and permanently ended their relationship. In the press, Keckley was harshly criticized for overstepping the line.

Elizabeth Keckley died in a home for destitute women in 1907. Ironically, as a successful businesswoman years earlier, she helped found the relief organization funding her home.

Section Five

They Overcame Hardship

Josephine Baker

By age twenty-one, Josephine Baker received 40,000 love letters and 2,000 proposals for marriage. Off stage, she strolled Paris with her pet cheetah, leopard, or swan, all on leashes. Albert Einstein, Picasso, E. E. Cummings, Ernest Hemingway, and architect Le Corbusier were her friends. She participated in the French Resistance against Nazi occupation during World War II, receiving the Croix de Guerre.

Baker's accomplishments are even more impressive considering her childhood. Born in St. Louis in 1906, Baker grew up in a one-room shack near Targee and Gratiot streets in the long-gone Mill Creek Valley neighborhood. She scavenged for coal near Union Station and food at Soulard Market. She begged for money on sidewalks.

Josephine Baker in 1949.
Courtesy Library of Congress

She tried but never succeeded as a dancer or singer in St. Louis. In 1919 at age thirteen, Baker left St. Louis.

She soon became the toast of Paris as an exotic dancer for *La Revue Negre*, the first African-American troupe to play the French capital. Baker entered the stage doing the splits upside down while carried on the shoulder of a giant. Her costume: one pink flamingo feather between the legs. Sometimes she danced the Charleston, and sometimes she strutted like an Egyptian pharaoh. Baker occasionally descended upon the stage inside a flower-covered globe. Wearing a banana miniskirt, she danced on a mirror tilted toward the audience. She always appeared with little clothing, very sensual and black, a rarity in Europe.

Audiences loved her. As much as she was depressed in St. Louis, Josephine Baker was exalted in Paris. Ironically, biographer Bennetta Jules-Rosette insists Baker's successful choreography in Paris must have been developed on stage in St. Louis.

The untrained girl from St. Louis took Paris by storm and became one of the highest paid entertainers in Europe by 1927. No flash in the pan, Baker remained among France's top entertainers for the next fifty years. Baker also entertained huge audiences in Prague, Berlin, Budapest, and Barcelona.

To understand, perhaps we need to have seen her. As one reviewer reflected after watching Josephine Baker's act, "The thought comes to mind—Sinatra thinks HE's a living legend? Go sit down, Frank. You aren't even close."

From Orphanage to the Governor's Mansion

Ted Kulongoski was born in St. Louis in 1940. His father died when he was a month old. When his mother gave up trying to raise him on her own in 1944, Ted was sent to St. Joseph's Home for Boys, an orphanage on South Grand Avenue where he would live for the next ten years.

Along with 200 other boys, Kulongoski was taught rules, responsibility, and consequences by the nuns at the orphanage. Group discipline resulted when one of the boys got out of line.

For Kulongoski, the experience was lonely. He later told the *Eugene Register Guard*, "at the orphanage (you) had nobody to kiss the hurts or put their arm around you and tell you you're gonna make it." He was one of the smaller boys and learned how to get along and survive. Years later, he remembered having to either fight or run fast— and Kulongoski admitted he was not a fast runner.

Ted Kulongoski. Courtesy State of Oregon

Disruptive in class and poor as a student, Kulongoski's future prospects seemed grim. But something in him appealed to teacher Bill Smith. Smith stood up for Kulongoski, encouraged him, and recommended he attend Missouri Boys State, a leadership program for promising high schoolers.

That's where things changed. Kulongoski won a Boys State Leadership competition. He was suddenly on track.

He served in Vietnam, worked in a steel mill, and then used the G.I. Bill to attend the University of Missouri where he also went to law school. He moved to Oregon where he served three years in the Oregon House, five in the senate, one term as attorney general, four years as an Oregon Supreme Court justice, and eight years as governor from 2003 to 2011.

Today, Ted Kulongoski, once a resident of the St. Joseph's Home for Boys in St. Louis, is the only governor to serve in all three branches of Oregon's government.

The Spinks Brothers

One of St. Louis's poorest neighborhoods—Darst-Webbe—produced two world heavyweight boxing champions, both from the same family.

Darst-Webbe was a federally subsidized public housing complex constructed in 1956. Bound by Fourteenth Street, Chouteau Avenue, South Tucker Boulevard, and Lafayette Avenue, it replaced a neighborhood of 515 homes, of which "362 had no toilets and 131 had no running water."

Darst-Webbe was immediately known for having too little room for too many residents and no access to shopping or jobs. But out of poverty came greatness in the form of Michael and Leon Spinks.

Leon (left) and Michael Spinks.

Both Spinks brothers won boxing gold medals in the 1976 Olympics, feats even more impressive considering Darst-Webbe was notorious for not having "enough recreational space."

With just seven professional bouts under his belt, twenty-four-year-old Leon Spinks took on, of all boxers, Muhammad Ali in Las Vegas in February 1978. Attacking Ali's kidneys and left shoulder, the kid from Darst-Webbe won the decision to take the heavyweight belt. Ali regained it six months later.

Leon's brother Michael was the light heavyweight champion who, with the help of St. Louis Cardinals shortstop Ozzie Smith's trainer Mackie Shillstone, gained twenty-five pounds to become a heavyweight contender. Weighing 200 pounds, he won the heavyweight championship by defeating the 220-pound Larry Holmes in a unanimous decision in 1985. He defeated Holmes again six months later but lost the title to Mike Tyson. He retired from boxing to care for his daughter whose mother had died in an accident.

Michael and Leon Spinks of St. Louis were the first brothers in boxing history to win heavyweight titles.

The "Ignominious" Start of Tennessee Williams

If you are struggling in school, please take a few moments to read this entry. If your kids are struggling in school, copy this entry and post it on the fridge. The following words are dedicated to those who are NOT the A students.

Perhaps you know of St. Louis playwright Tennessee Williams. He grew up in St. Louis during the first half of the twentieth century. Williams did not get off to a great start. He wrote poetry—which his father referred to as "nonsense"—at Ben Blewett Junior High in University City. He attended the University of Missouri and got Bs and Cs. Because of the poor grades, his dad pulled him out of college and put him to work  in the International Shoe factory, which he found boring.

In 1937, at age twenty-six, he was still in college. Williams submitted a play, *Death of Pierrot*, in the Webster Groves Play Contest. He lost. He wrote to a friend, "I got eliminated from the Webster Groves Play Contest. . . . The thought is disturbing. I would like (almost) to put a stick of dynamite under their damned old play tonight. Yes, I'm still very touchy about such things. They hit me where it hurts most."

One might assume Tennessee Williams would ace his English courses. But as a senior at Washington University during the spring of 1937, he got a B in English 16, a course involving technique in modern drama.

The course required students to compete in a contest by writing and reading aloud their original plays. An independent jury was established to select the three best, which would be staged. Of those, a winner would be selected and its author would receive fifty dollars. Williams submitted *Me, Vashya*. As he read it in class, there was "stifled laughter."

The play came in fourth place. Williams wrote in his diary, "Never a more ignominious failure! . . . it does hurt to get a direct kick in the face like that and if there is any guts left in me I'll make up for it in some way. It looks like I'm on the way down. . . ."

But Williams was wrong—he was on the way up.

He turned his boring International Shoe work into a positive. Fellow factory worker Stanley Kowalski became a character in *A Streetcar Named Desire*. Williams turned another co-worker, Jim Connor, into the gentleman caller Jim O'Connor in *A Glass Menagerie*.

Later, this mediocre student would win four Drama Critic Circle Awards, two Pulitzer Prizes, and the Presidential Medal of Freedom!

He was hailed as "brilliant and prolific." Others said he was "one of the greatest playwrights in American history." He was also called "one of America's greatest artists."

The winner of the Washington University playwriting class was Aaron (A. E.) Hotchner, who later became Ernest Hemingway's biographer, the author of *King of the Hill*, and a partner with actor Paul Newman in a line of not-for-profit salad dressings.

Tennessee WIlliam (right) speaking with Andy Warhol. Courtesy Library of Congress

So, for you students getting Bs and Cs and rejections in your chosen field, learn from Tennessee Williams: Don't listen to others and in a couple years we'll be writing about you!

Joseph Conway's Story; or, Why I Will Never Complain About Anything Again

How difficult was life in the eighteenth century? Very. Let's take, for example, the story of Joseph Conway.

Born in Virginia in 1763, Conway was sixteen when Indians in Kentucky "scalped" him. "The blood ran down his back from the scalp wounds," according to one story. Family accounts indicated his wounds were treated with the most advanced medicine available at the time: wads of cobwebs made into a poultice to stanch the bleeding.

And that was just one incident.

On another occasion, he was captured by Indians near the Ohio River and forced to walk barefoot to Detroit. This was a distance of about 350 miles, or 117 days by foot using modern roads, which did not exist back then, of course. He was held in a prison on the Canadian border for four years.

> *Ripley's Believe It or Not* claimed Conway was … scalped three times, tomahawked three times, shot three times, left for dead three times …

He moved to St. Louis in 1798. Boys would gather behind him to see the scars on his head. His St. Louis home stood at what is today White and Conway roads in Chesterfield. Conway Road is named in his honor.

Ulysses S. Grant–
The Greatest Comeback

Feeling down? Convinced you'll never succeed? Please read about a St. Louisan who once felt the same way and ended up doing just fine.

In 1854, seven years before the start of the Civil War, Ulysses S. Grant resigned from the army because he wanted to be closer to his wife, Julia, and their children in St. Louis. Also, his superiors were concerned about his drinking.

Grant, a West Point graduate, had no means to support his family. According to historian H. W. Brands, Grant was not sure Julia wanted him around. Her recent letters had been cold and infrequent.

Before arriving in St. Louis, Grant was "poor and forlorn." He stopped in New York and then Ohio to see family. His father, Jesse, was disappointed to learn of his son's army resignation. Grant asked to work in the family's leather business in Illinois, but his father would allow it only if Julia and the boys stayed in Missouri. Why? He didn't want to build them a house. Grant refused his father's terms and moved to St. Louis. He built a log cabin, but his wife called it "crude and homely." She preferred living on her father's more upscale property.

In the winter of 1854–55, Grant worked on his farm. By 1856, he needed money for seeds, labor, and horses. He wrote his father asking for money. The request was rejected.

"I have worked hard but got little," the younger Grant lamented.

He wrote his father again, "It is always usual for parents to give their children assistance in beginning life (and I am only beginning, though thirty-five years of age, nearly) and what I ask is not much."

His father still sent no money.

Grant worked night and day. Money was tight. He hired one slave but could have used a lot more help. A neighbor's slave said, "I have seen many farmers, but I never saw one that worked harder than Mr. Grant."

Ironically, the harder he worked in St. Louis, the less respect he received from neighbors. In slave states, the gentry did not perform undignified farm duties. Such was work for slaves, servants, and hired hands. Neighbors' opinions did not matter to him, but they did to Mrs. Grant, a St. Louis native. With so little money, Julia did not even have the proper shoes to go shopping.

In December 1857, Ulysses pawned his gold watch for twenty-two dollars. He gave up on his farm and instead worked the farm owned by Julia's father, who "openly despised" his son-in-law.

In 1858, Grant joined Harry Boggs in a real estate venture. Because their offices were in downtown St. Louis and some distance from the Dent farm, Boggs allowed Grant to spend weeknights in an unfinished backroom with a bed, pitcher, and bowl. Business was bad due to the Panic

General Ulysses S. Grant. Courtesy Library of Congress

Grant and Buckner

On his way back to St. Louis after resigning from the army in 1854, Ulysses Grant stopped in New York. Penniless, he asked for and received a loan from Simon Bolivar Buckner, his old friend from West Point and the Mexican War.

Grant's first victory in the Civil War took place on February 16, 1862, at Fort Donelson. Grant was not generous with his terms for the surrendering enemy. "No terms except an unconditional and immediate surrender can be accepted," he famously insisted. The surrendering Confederate general found Grant to be "ungenerous and unchivalrous." Ironically, that general was Simon Bolivar Buckner. Buckner did not hold a grudge. He served as a pallbearer at Grant's funeral in 1885.

of 1857. Boggs's wife, Louisa, described a depressed Grant: "He sat humbly by my fireside. He had no exalted opinion of himself at any time . . . he seemed almost in despair."

When Boggs traveled out of town on business, he left Grant in charge of the office. Upon returning, he found the business in shambles. "The books were in confusion, the wrong people had been let into houses." Grant was fired. Louisa said, ". . . he was a sad man."

Grant applied for a job as the St. Louis County engineer. His application was rejected. In 1860, he wrote his father about the rejection. The two agreed he would move to Galena and work in the family business.

A year later, the outbreak of the Civil War drew him back to the military. He would lead the North to victory. Ulysses Grant, the failed St. Louis farmer and businessman, was elected president of the United States in 1868 and 1872.

Caray and Hotchner

And now for something completely different: I found two St. Louis autobiographies that share eerily similar anecdotes. See if you find this as weird as I do.

Let's start with Harry Caray, maybe the most famous Cardinals announcer in team history. Caray also became nationally famous for calling the Cubs games on WGN.

Caray grew up in St. Louis and attended Dewey Elementary School. On Caray's grade-school graduation day in 1928, all the boys wore blue blazers and white pants—except Caray. Too poor to afford white pants, Caray wore his regular grey slacks instead.

In his autobiography, *Holy Cow*, Caray describes the humiliation he felt that day when the other boys made fun of him for wearing grey—not white—slacks. "The other kids really gave it to me," he wrote in 1989. "They badgered and ridiculed—and believe me, nothing is crueler than the humor of young children. They couldn't possibly have known the hurt, the embarrassment, I felt."

As a strange coincidence, author A. E. Hotchner had an almost identical experience. Hotchner is the author of many books and plays, including *Papa Hemingway* and *Sophia, Living and Loving*. With the late actor Paul Newman, Hotchner cofounded Newman's Own, Inc.

In his memoir, *King of the Hill*, Hotchner also describes the ridicule he encountered on graduation day from the same Dewey School six years later. Why was Hotchner laughed at?

For the same reason as Caray: his clothes.

At a party on graduation day, the other boys sneered at Hotchner's oversized, borrowed blazer. Like Caray, Hotchner had no money for a graduation outfit so he borrowed a coat that was too big and a shirt that was too tight. When using the restroom, Hotchner overheard the other boys laughing at his wardrobe.

"Hey, did you see that jacket (Hotchner) is wearing?"

"That's not his jacket, that's his overcoat."

"Maybe he thinks it's a costume party."

"He'd win first prize, all right."

Hotchner wrote, "They all had a good laugh. . . . I waited until I was sure they were all gone before I came out. All the way home I kept telling myself I didn't care what they thought of my jacket and shirt. . . ."

Yet Hotchner cared enough to include the story almost forty years later in his 1972 memoir. The Dewey School graduation must have impacted Caray as well, for he too included it in his autobiography sixty-one years later.

Let's go over this again: two St. Louisans—both poor with cheap clothing, and both from the same grade school—experienced the same humiliation in front of peers at graduation. Both wrote about it years later after they became famous.

Coincidence?

Harry Caray in the broadcast booth with Gabby Street

HARRY CARAY   GABBY STREET

Section Six

I Didn't Know There Was a St. Louis Connection

Cats

The second-longest-running Broadway musical—and the fourth-longest-running show in London's West End—has roots in St. Louis. *Cats* is based on the poetry in *Old Possum's Book of Practical Cats* by T. S. Eliot, who was reared in St. Louis. Andrew Lloyd Webber, creator of *Cats*, grew up reading Eliot.

The musical's characters—Mr. Mistoffelees, Old Deuteronomy, Jellicles, Macavity, Gus, etc.—are all cats from the book. Webber also included some of Eliot's unpublished verses such as "Grizabella the Glamour Cat," a poem given to him by Eliot's widow, Valerie, in 1980. Grizabella sings the production's showstopper, *Memory*.

Who was Eliot? Sometimes called the greatest poet of the modern era and one of the most influential writers in the English language, T. S. Eliot was born on September 26, 1888, in a house at 2635 Locust Street. His youth here shaped him greatly. He told the *St. Louis Post-Dispatch* in 1930, "Missouri and the Mississippi have made a deeper impression on me than any other part of the world."

Prufrock, a furniture store located at both 1104 Olive Street and 422 N. Fourth Street inspired the title of one of Eliot's most famous poems, "The Love Song of J. Alfred Prufrock." The poem's "yellow fog" refers to the smog of St. Louis factories.

In 1914, Eliot moved to Great Britain and eventually became a British subject. He won the Nobel Prize in Literature in 1948.

Eliot did not come from a family of slackers: his grandfather founded Washington University.

Francesca Simon

T. S. Eliot was not the only St. Louisan to become a major writer in the United Kingdom. Francesca Simon was born in St. Louis in 1955. Her family lived in Vinita Park.

Her father, Mayo Simon, worked at KETC-TV. Among other things, he directed the show *The Religions of Man*, hosted by Huston Smith. The family moved from St. Louis to Los Angeles, where Mayo wrote the screenplays for *Marooned*, *Futureworld*, and other movies.

Francesca moved to London and created the Horrid Henry series of books for children. She was the eighteenth bestselling author in the United Kingdom from 2000 to 2009, according to *The Telegraph*. Horrid Henry has also been turned into a television show and a play in London's West End.

Simon has sold 18 million Horrid Henry books. In 2008, she was the first American to win the British Book Award for the Children's Book of the Year.

A Chorus Line

A St. Louisan changed the conclusion of one of the world's most famous musicals, *A Chorus Line*.

Webster Groves's Marsha Mason, who studied at Nerinx Hall High School and Webster College, became a celebrated actress best known for her Oscar-nominated work in *The Goodbye Girl* with Richard Dreyfuss.

In 1975, she attended a preview of the musical *A Chorus Line* with her husband, the playwright Neil Simon. *A Chorus Line* examines the lives of actors and actresses auditioning for a Broadway show. After viewing the production, Mason told director Michael Bennett she felt the show was a "downer."

Why? Because an older character, Cassie, trying to revive her career, was cut at the end of the show. Mason felt audiences would root for Cassie. Her success would give people hope. If Cassie was rejected, the audience would leave the theater sad. Bennett balked. He wanted his show to reflect the brutal realities of show business.

But Mason insisted, "You don't go to the theater to experience real life. You go to the theater to be inspired, to hope, to change, to be in touch with your emotions on a positive level."

Mason told Bennett Cassie had to succeed in her audition. Bennett listened to Mason and changed the script. Anyone who has seen the show knows the revision completely altered the mood of the production's ending.

When *A Chorus Line* opened on Broadway in 1975, the character Cassie got a part in the show. The musical, created by Michael Bennett—with assistance from Marsha Mason!— broke all box office records and is still performed today.

How a Jerk from St. Louis Made Sure We Got Beautiful Music

Composer Burt Bacharach was working in 1968 with an all-star group to create the musical *Promises, Promises* for Broadway. His group included lyricist Hal David, choreographer Michael Bennett, and writer Neil Simon. Creative teams don't get any better.

But producer David Merrick was not happy with the team. Merrick was a St. Louisan whose first job in show business was selling ice cream at the Muny. He became a top Broadway executive by producing *Gypsy, Cactus Flower, Irma La Douce, Hello Dolly!, 42nd Street,* and others. He disliked St. Louis so much he once returned an honorary key to the city. Merrick refused to fly TWA because it made stops at Lambert Airport, which was, of course, in St. Louis.

"David Merrick was not one of the nicest guys in the world, to say the least," said Burt Bacharach.

As *Promises, Promises* was previewing in Boston, the creative team of Bacharach, David, Simon, and Bennett gathered in the restroom. Merrick busted in and yelled, "If you think this friggin' show is going to work, you're out of your minds."

He turned to Bacharach, "We're missing a song in the middle of the second act, and what we need is something the audience can whistle on their way out of the theater." According to one account, Bennett went into a stall and just started sobbing.

Bacharach fell ill and ended up in Massachusetts General Hospital. Merrick relentlessly called him for new music. He even offered to send a piano to Bacharach's hospital room.

Inspired by Bacharach's illness, David wrote the lyrics, "What do you do when you kiss a guy? / You get enough germs to catch pneumonia / After you do, he'll never phone ya."

Still ill, Bacharach took the lyrics and wrote the music for "I'll Never Fall in Love Again." He wrote the song faster than he had ever written any song in his life. It became "the outstanding hit from the score and pretty much stopped the show every night."

"I'll Never Fall in Love Again" was recorded by Dionne Warwick and reached No. 6 on the Billboard Charts in 1970.

Would we have this musical treasure if David Merrick had been a nice guy?

Colin Firth in St. Louis

Academy Award–winning British actor Colin Firth is known for his roles in *The King's Speech*, *Love Actually*, *Bridget Jones's Diary*, and *Shakespeare in Love*, among others. He is not known for living in St. Louis. But he did.

Colin Firth lived on Gold Finch Drive in Florissant in 1972 and 1973 and attended Hazelwood West Junior High School. At the same time, a Florissant family lived in the Firth family home in England as part of an international exchange. Firth's father taught at Florissant Valley Community College while here.

According to biographer Sandro Monetti, the school experience in St. Louis was "hideous." His English accent set him apart from his classmates. He was put in classes with older students. Other kids used drugs while he played with train sets. They wore combat jackets, and he was just out of short trousers. To escape it all, he buried himself in books.

But Firth's St. Louis experience was not all bad. In a 2010 interview with the *St. Louis Post-Dispatch*'s Calvin Wilson, Firth remembered falling in love with classical music when he heard Beethoven's Ninth performed under the Arch.

Firth later revisited St. Louis after finding success and fame in the movies. He tried to visit his old school but was turned away at the door by administrators. They didn't recognize him.

Tom Cruise in St. Louis

One of Hollywood's most bankable stars not only lived in St. Louis as a kid, but also decided to become an actor while here.

Tom Cruise, known then as Tommy Mapother, lived at the corner of Fernway Lane and Fernpark Drive in Creve Coeur in the 1960s. His father, Thomas Cruise Mapother III, was an electrical engineer, and his mother, Mary Lee Mapother, taught dyslexic and hyperkinetic children and was an amateur actress.

In 2005, Cruise told *60 Minutes* in Australia, "I wanted to be an actor when I was about four years old. Yeah, four years old was the first time I thought of being an actor. I was living in St. Louis. That was the first time I thought about being an actor."

The Mapothers moved frequently and left St. Louis after several years.

The Lordi family lived behind the Mapothers. Teenagers Sue and Barb Lordi babysat Tom and his three sisters. Fifty years later, Sue remembered Mary Lee as a fun, outgoing woman who came across the backyard to smoke cigarettes and talk over coffee. She remembers Tommy Mapother as "mischievous."

Darth Vader Got His Start in St. Louis

Actor James Earl Jones grew up in Michigan, but he spent summers in his youth in St. Louis with relatives. He saw his first live stage performance—*Naughty Marietta*—at the Muny in 1944. In his autobiography, he described the event as "bliss."

Jones must have been bitten by the acting bug. He later starred on Broadway in *Othello* and *The Great White Hope*. He later acted in films such as *Dr. Strangelove* and *Field of Dreams*.

Although today Jones is famous for providing the voices of *The Lion King* and Darth Vader in *Star Wars*, he stuttered as a child. Taking the advice of a teacher, Jones cured his problem by reading Shakespeare aloud.

Jean Lafitte: The Pirate Who Saved St. Louis

In the War of 1812, the British Navy sought to shut down all ports on America's East Coast and capture New Orleans. From there, the British planned to move up the Mississippi River, join with their own forces in Canada, and then "shove the Americans into the Atlantic Ocean."

The first objective was accomplished by 1814 when the British blockaded all U.S. seaports from the Atlantic to the Gulf Coast. After burning most of Washington, including the White House, the British descended upon New Orleans under the direction of Colonel Edward Nicholls.

Nicholls's strategy took a strange turn at New Orleans. He solicited the military assistance of Jean Lafitte and his band of bandana-and-pantaloon-clad pirates working out of Barataria Bay near New Orleans. According to historian Winston Groom, Nicholls offered Lafitte a full pardon, British citizenship, land, and about $2 million (current value) for his assistance.

Jean Lafitte, a handsome, well-dressed Frenchman born in Port-au-Prince, Haiti, around 1782, was not technically a pirate. Unlike pirates, who pretty much targeted any vessel for loot, Lafitte operated as a "privateer"; he only captured ships flying the flags of countries at war with his own. Lafitte's privateers seized mostly Spanish and British vessels and auctioned the loot in New Orleans. In addition to vessels, Lafitte commanded an almost inexhaustible supply of munitions—cannons, gunpowder, artillery—hidden in Gulf Coast swamps.

Lafitte not only rejected Nicholls's offer, but he went a

step further by notifying New Orleans about the forthcoming British invasion. He also offered his services to General Andrew Jackson's army, which was moving from Mobile to defend New Orleans.

Nobody knows why Lafitte rejected the British request. Perhaps he felt America was his adopted homeland. Or, as historian Groom suggests, Lafitte thought if he spurned Britain the United States would forgive him for past smuggling and looting.

It was a miscalculation. Both the state of Louisiana and General Jackson rejected Lafitte. What's more, American troops cracked down on Lafitte's camp on September 14, 1814, and seized his ships and loot.

Lafitte escaped capture and hid. Now he had two armies mad at him.

Three months later, Lafitte's status improved when the Americans suffered setbacks at a battle on Lake Borgne. Knowing Lafitte had lots of weapons and ammunition, General Jackson finally agreed to accept help from Lafitte and his buccaneers.

It was a good move for Jackson.

At the Battle of New Orleans, Jackson's army prevailed in no small measure thanks to Lafitte. Lafitte's brother and cousin commanded detachments. Serving as Jackson's aide-de-camp, Lafitte instructed Jackson to strengthen a parapet protecting New Orleans from the advancing British—advice that proved to be "the best Jackson received during the entire battle."

Jackson's army, unlike the Brits, had access to munitions and manpower from Lafitte. With his fellow privateers firing cannons and artillery, Lafitte helped defeat the British troops. Gone now was the British plan to control the Mississippi River, including St. Louis.

On January 21, 1815, Jackson's army paraded in New Orleans with Lafitte's buccaneers. On February 6, Lafitte and his comrades were pardoned for crimes by President James Madison. Lafitte continued his privateering, first in New Orleans and then in Galveston.

And what happened to Lafitte?

He left Galveston in 1821. A journal supposedly written by Lafitte suggests he then moved to St. Louis, changed his name to John Lafflin, married a woman named Emma Mortimere, and then settled down, eventually spending his last days in Alton, Illinois, before dying in 1854.

Groom poses the question: What if Lafitte had sided with Great Britain? Would Andrew Jackson have won the Battle of New Orleans? If not, would the British have moved up the Mississippi River and seized St. Louis?

Did a pirate save St. Louis?

The Serenity Prayer

One of the most famous prayers was written by a St. Louisan.

Protestant theologian Reinhold Niebuhr was born in Wright City, just outside of St. Louis, on June 21, 1892. He attended Eden Seminary in St. Louis but left around 1913 when his father died suddenly.

He is credited with authoring the Serenity Prayer as early as 1937. The prayer has been used by the USO and Alcoholics Anonymous. The best known version of the prayer is:

God, grant me the serenity to accept the things I cannot change,
The courage to change the things I can,
And wisdom to know the difference.

Niebuhr greatly influenced theologians, political thinkers, and presidents. "He's one of my favorite philosophers," said President Barack Obama.

Oldest Surviving Recording of a Human Voice

In 1878, inventor Thomas Edison visited St. Louis to demonstrate a tinfoil phonograph. At the event, St. Louis newspaper writer Thomas Mason, who went by the pen name I. X. Peck, recited poems "Old Mother Hubbard" and "Mary Had a Little Lamb" on Edison's new equipment. Mason forgot some of the lines, but that was okay. The point of the session was to show the promise of recording equipment. Sadly, Mason died three weeks later from sunstroke during a St. Louis heat wave.

In 2012, historians at the Museum of Innovation and Science in Schenectady discovered the 1878 recording and developed a computer program to restore it.

Today, Mason's seventy-eight-second sound bite is the oldest surviving recording of a human voice. And, the earliest recorded blooper as well.

The Allman Brothers

The Allman Brothers—considered "the principal architects of Southern Rock"—rank among rock and roll's greatest performing groups. With ten gold albums, including four certified platinum, Duane Allman, Gregg Allman, and Dickie Betts paved the way for bands like Charlie Daniels, Marshall Tucker, and Lynyrd Skynyrd.

It's not widely known the Allmans played in St. Louis's Gaslight Square for twenty-eight weeks in 1967. Performing at Pepe's a Go Go, the brothers were known then as the Allman Joys. Gregg Allman remembers, "They had dancing girls in cages and the bandstand was on stilts on top of the dance floor. We played six nights a week, five sets a night, 45 minutes a set for $444 a week."

Allman recalls Pepe's hospitable owner bringing the band food and allowing them to play in the club all night long. In St. Louis, the Allmans worked on various songs, such as "Stormy Monday," later included in *At Fillmore East*, the band's breakthrough 1971 album considered one of rock's greatest.

In his memoir, Gregg Allman described Gaslight Square as "this little slice of town, kind of like Bourbon Street. It was just one street and all the dens of iniquity were there."

The Nitty Gritty Dirt Band came to St. Louis in 1967 and played the Kiel Auditorium. After the show, they dropped into Pepe's for a beer and "were knocked out" by the Allman Joys. Their manager Bill McEuen recommended the Allmans move to Los Angeles.

Gregg objected but his older brother Duane "just wanted to get the '@#!?' out of St. Louis." The band left town.

The St. Louis Connection to "Double Vision"

"Double Vision," a hit song by the rock group Foreigner, was inspired by former St. Louis Blues hockey player and executive John Davidson. Lou Gramm, Foreigner's lead singer, was writing songs in a recording studio while the New York Rangers were playing the Philadelphia Flyers. Gramm followed the game on a small TV in the studio.

Davidson, then goaltending for the Rangers, got hit in the head. The announcer said, "Davidson will be fine, but he might have double vision."

Gramm knew instantly he had the needed lyrics for a new song. He shut off the TV and began writing "Double Vision."

The song reached No. 2 on the Billboard Charts.

Davidson, a first-round draft choice for the Blues in 1973, was the team's president from 2006 until 2012.

Guess Who Saved St. Louis's Harbor?

In 1838, sediment was building up on the St. Louis side of the Mississippi River. If left alone, the silt would have prevented boats from mooring in St. Louis's harbor. Local commerce would have been destroyed.

The Army Corps of Engineers sent a young lieutenant, and trained engineer, from Virginia to rectify the situation. The engineer designed a dam and dyke system that redirected the water's current to erase the sandbar threatening the harbor. This infrastructure still works: Russell Errett, hydraulic engineer with the U.S. Army Corps of Engineers, says those 1838 structures continue to maintain the river's navigation channel.

The name of the engineer: Robert E. Lee. Twenty-four years later, Lee would serve as commander of all Confederate troops in the Civil War.

Ironically, St. Louis, a Union city, was saved by a Confederate general!

Reddi-wip

St. Louis is also the home of . . . drum roll . . . whipped cream in a can. Invented by St. Louis businessman Bunny Lapin in 1946, Reddi-wip was first delivered to St. Louis homes by milkmen. Prior to Reddi-wip, aerosol cans were mostly used to dispense pesticides.

The product spread nationally, and by 1951 Lapin's Reddi-wip, Inc., had 750 employees and annual sales of $7 million. A trade publication reported Reddi-wip made Lapin wealthy: "He bought Cadillacs two at a time and lived in Gloria Swanson's furnished mansion in Hollywood." He also owned homes in St. Louis, Miami, and New York.

Time magazine called Lapin one of the twentieth century's most important inventors. Born in St. Louis in 1914, Lapin had a law degree from Washington University School of Law. At the time of his death, Reddi-wip represented one out of every two food toppings sold in a spray can.

The Birthplace of Peanut Butter

Did peanut butter originate in St. Louis? It seems so, according to John Krampner, author of *Creamy and Crunchy: An Informal History of Peanut Butter, the All-American Food.*

The staple food started with George Bayle, a Philadelphia native who moved to Alton, Illinois, in the 1870s to become a traveling cracker salesman. He started the George A. Bayle Company at 111 South Second Street in St. Louis around 1888.

Working in tandem with a local doctor in 1890, Bayle developed peanut butter for patients who needed protein but could not chew meat. The name of the doctor is unknown. Bayle's peanut butter sold for six cents a pound.

This version of events is corroborated by the Southern Peanut Growers trade association. The group's website claims Bayle and the St. Louis physician invented peanut butter in 1890 and then the Kellogg brothers of Battle Creek, Michigan, came up with a peanut butter preparation process in 1895.

Having said that, Krampner also suggests the possibility there was never a doctor involved. This alternative theory maintains Bayle sold peanut butter after failing to successfully market a peanut and cheese concoction.

Here's where the peanut butter story gets . . . sticky. Some, especially those tied to the Kellogg Company, credit the Kellogg brothers with inventing peanut butter, since they took out the first peanut butter patents. However, Krampner, citing the research of food historian Suzanne Corbett, concludes, "Kellogg's ground peanut paste probably bore only a cursory similarity to today's peanut butter." The Kelloggs steamed the peanuts, while Bayle—like today's modern peanut butter processors—roasted them.

The Bayle Company ran advertisements in the 1921 and 1922 editions of *The Peanut Promoter*, an industry publication, claiming to be the "Original Manufacturers of Peanut Butter." According to Krampner, nobody wrote the magazine disputing the claim.

Thus, St. Louis put the pb in pb and j. *Spread* the word!

O'Hare Airport

How many Cubs fans know their airport is named for a St. Louisan?

Holy cow . . . it's true.

Edward Henry "Butch" O'Hare was born in St. Louis in 1914. His parents split when he was a boy. His father moved to Chicago while Butch and his mother remained in Holly Hills. He attended Western Military Academy in Alton.

His father, Eddie, a graduate of Saint Louis University Law School, started doing business with mobster Al Capone in Chicago. He later gave the IRS Capone's financial records, a move that led to the gangster's conviction and incarceration for tax evasion. As a result, Eddie O'Hare Sr. was gunned down in Chicago by Capone loyalists on November 8, 1939.

Meanwhile, Eddie Jr. began flight training at the Naval Air Station at Pensacola, Florida. He became a Navy pilot. And on February 20, 1942, he took on a squadron of Japanese bombers—although outnumbered nine to one—and prevailed, shooting down five Japanese bombers in about four minutes.

Two months later, President Franklin Roosevelt awarded

Butch O'Hare's father, Eddie, decided to turn on Al Capone at a secret 1930 meeting with IRS official Frank Wilson at the Missouri Athletic Club in downtown St. Louis. The get-together was arranged by John Rogers, a reporter for the *St. Louis Post-Dispatch*. Yes, St. Louisans put in motion and were responsible for the undoing of Chicago's most notorious gangster, Al Capone.

O'Hare the U.S. Medal of Honor. He was its first naval recipient in World War II.

Sixty thousand attended a homecoming parade held in O'Hare's honor in St. Louis.

However, on November 26, 1943, O'Hare was shot down by the Japanese in the Pacific. On December 20, 1943, his funeral mass was held at the New Cathedral in St. Louis.

Colonel Robert McCormick, editor and publisher of the *Chicago Tribune*, suggested his city name its airport after O'Hare. Throwing the might of his newspaper behind his idea, McCormick succeeded and the airport became O'Hare Field, Chicago International Airport on September 17, 1949.

The world's fifth busiest airport is named after a war hero from St. Louis who never lived in Chicago!

A St. Louis Tomb That Inspired One of the Nation's Most Famous Homes

Visitors from all over the world flock to see the home and studio of the late world-renowned architect Frank Lloyd Wright in Oak Park, Illinois. Experts consider it one of the most architecturally significant homes in the United States.

It turns out Wright "borrowed" a small architectural element from a St. Louis mausoleum. According to the home's tour guides, Wright modeled his master bedroom's T-shaped windows after the design used by Wright's boss, the noted architect Louis Sullivan, in the Wainwright Tomb in Bellefontaine Cemetery in St. Louis.

The World Leader Who Operated a St. Louis Forklift

Former French President Jacques Chirac worked in St. Louis in 1953.

In 2003, when accused of not liking the United States and its plans to invade Iraq, Chirac denied he was anti-American.

Au contraire, Chirac explained to *Time* magazine, "I've known the U.S. for a long time. I visit often, I've studied there, worked as a forklift operator for Anheuser-Busch in St. Louis . . . and I really like the United States."

St. Louis may have been in his past, but it was not forgotten.

"I still like a Bud," he told Barbara Slavin of *USA Today*.

Vive St. Louis!

(Where world leaders operate forklifts.)

Angels in America

When most St. Louisans mention angels, they are usually singing Christmas songs or badmouthing Albert Pujols. St. Louis, however, has another angels connection.

The play *Angels in America*, winner of the Pulitzer Prize and numerous Tony Awards, was born in St. Louis.

Dramatist Tony Kushner was at the Repertory Theatre of St. Louis on a National Endowment for the Arts directing fellowship in 1984–85. While here, Kushner wrote a poem, *Angels in America*, highlighting what he believed to be a Mormon contradiction between good works and biased beliefs.

It was his first idea for the play, which he began to write in 1987. Divided into two parts, *Angels in America* won the Tony Award for Best Play in 1993 and 1994.

And if you really want to wave the St. Louis flag on this one, just remember the show was produced on Broadway by Rocco Landesman, a Clayton native.

Birthplace of Halitosis

Just about everyone is familiar with Listerine mouthwash. If there was a Hall of Fame for products made in St. Louis, Listerine would be in it. However, Listerine was sold for almost forty years before it was marketed as an antidote to bad breath.

First, a little background: Listerine was invented by St. Louisan J. W. Lambert in 1884 as a disinfectant for surgical procedures. With an office and factory at 2101 Locust Street, Lambert Pharmacal Company later marketed Listerine as an oral antiseptic to the dental community.

In 1922, however, Listerine sales needed a boost. Lambert's son Gerard, the firm's general manager, called a meeting at the company's St. Louis offices and said nobody would leave the room until someone came up with an advertising idea for Listerine.

Ideas were tossed around. Gerard's brother Marion spoke up.

"How about bad breath?" he asked.

Gerard later wrote, "I glared, reminding him this was a respectable meeting."

Bad breath was, in 1922, an inappropriate topic for polite conversation let alone a national marketing campaign. But an older member of Lambert's staff, Arthur Deacon, produced an article from the British medical journal *The Lancet*, which used the word "halitosis," to describe smelly breath. Nobody in the room had heard of this medical term, but everyone agreed "halitosis" would provide a respectable cover for Lambert Pharmacal Company's new ad campaign against bad breath.

Bad breath was not a major concern in 1922, a time when many people bathed just once a week. So Gerard Lambert and his Chicago ad agency, Williams and Cunningham, crafted an advertisement with the headline "Often a Bridesmaid but Never a Bride" with accompanying copy describing a woman possessing all the world's advantages but never succeeding because of "halitosis." Another ad warned, "Even Your Best Friend Won't Tell You."

Employees at the ad agency were polled, and 82 percent predicted the ads would fail. Nonetheless, the "halitosis" ads ran in 300 newspapers and 80 magazines.

Within five years, Lambert was spending $5 million annually on halitosis advertising. Americans started to become self-conscious about their breath, a concern they had not previously

Speaking of social embarrassment, Gerard Lambert's daughter Bunny Lambert Mellon would later achieve notoriety for giving U.S. Senator John Edwards hundreds of thousands of dollars during the 2008 presidential campaign. Edwards was accused of using the money to hide his pregnant mistress.

had. Listerine was soon netting $4 million a year in profits.

Eventually, "halitosis" appeared in all dictionaries. Lambert later wrote he feared his tombstone would read, "Here Lies the Father of Halitosis."

> Today, the Listerine website credits Gerard Lambert as the man in St. Louis who introduced Americans to halitosis.

DON'T FOOL YOUR SELF

Since halitosis never announces itself, to the victim, you simply cannot know when you have it.

Original LISTERINE
MOUTHWASH
Helps fight germs that cause Bad Breath
Plaque & Gum problems

Halitosis makes *you unpopular*

It is unexcusable . . . can be instantly remedied

Animal House

Animal House, the 1978 comedy about college frat life starring the late John Belushi, was co-written by Harold Ramis, a 1966 graduate of Washington University in St. Louis and a member of the school's Zeta Beta Tau fraternity.

Did actual ZBT frat boys at Washington University resemble those in the movie?

Here's the entry for ZBT in the 1966 edition of *The Hatchet*, the Wash U yearbook:

"Never before have so few 'Zeb's' contributed so little to campus activities. Caught between the innate instinct to not give a care about the campus and the natural inclination toward academic achievement shown by our brothers; we feel we must extend our deepest personal gratitude to Jack Wides and Gary Friedman who 'cared enough to do their very best' for both Zeta Beta Tau and Hatchet. Their discovery (on the night before the last shipment of Hatchet went off to the publishers) that only seventeen ZBT's had bothered to have their pictures taken, saved the day and possibly the face for the fraternity. After all, we know that there are more than seventeen ZBT's: what we often wonder is if more than seventeen care."

Judge for yourself.

St. Louis's Frequent Visitor: Ray Charles

For about thirty years, one of the country's top recording artists slipped unnoticed into St. Louis for romantic liaisons.

Ray Charles, known for hits like "Hit the Road Jack," "Georgia On My Mind," "I Can't Stop Loving You," and "What'd I Say," started a longtime relationship with Kirkwood divorcee Marci Soto in 1968.

According to Soto's 2011 memoir *Ray and Me*, the two spent lots of time at various St. Louis restaurants, including the Charcoal House, White Castle, the Red Lobster on South Lindbergh, Al Baker's, and the Frontenac Hilton (formerly known as the Breckenridge Frontenac).

Soto, who runs a house cleaning service, chronicled the affair with photos, sound recordings, and videotape.

Buzz Bissinger

Life's profound moments come at unexpected times. Just ask Pulitzer Prize–winning author Buzz Bissinger. Bissinger is known for serious, critically acclaimed works like *Friday Night Lights, Three Nights in August,* and *Shattered Glass.*

So where would Bissinger experience one of his "most powerful moments in life?"

Mt. Everest? The Grand Canyon? The Western Wall in Jerusalem?

Here's the story:

Bissinger and his son Zach—a disabled man living with brain damage since birth—roamed the country by car during a 2009 road trip. The two—who never bonded extremely well due to Buzz's personality and Zach's disability—stopped at Six Flags in St. Louis.

They decided to ride the Dragon's Wing, a 153-foot free fall similar to a bungee jump, but for two people, not one. Scared beyond belief, the Bissingers took the leap and hugged each other as tightly as possible on the way down.

Buzz later recalled, "I will never forget it. It was a beautiful, exquisite moment. A spiritual bonding. I had never held him so tightly. He had never held me that way. It was the most powerful physical moment that I've ever had."

In *Father's Day,* he wrote, "For the first time in my life I feel that Zach and I share the same mental ground, think the same way, seize the world on equal terms." Yes, a poignant, powerful father-son bonding occurs unexpectedly for a Pulitzer Prize journalist . . . on a ride at Six Flags in St. Louis.

It can happen.

Southern Comfort

M. W. Heron was born in St. Louis in 1850. As a bartender in New Orleans in 1874, he was asked to improve the quality of some whiskey gone bad. Heron added fruit and spices to the whiskey and called it Cuffs and Buttons.

In an attempt to make Heron's liqueur appealing to customers in the South, the name was changed to Southern Comfort. He gave it a subtitle, "The Grand Old Drink of the South."

Heron later owned a bar at 319 Pine Street in downtown St. Louis. Southern Comfort won a gold medal at the 1904 World's Fair.

What did M. W. stand for? Martin Wilkes. The theory goes Heron preferred to use only his initials after President Lincoln was assassinated by John Wilkes Booth.

Heron died in St. Louis three months after Prohibition began on April 17, 1920. He is buried in Calvary Cemetery. Today, every bottle of Southern Comfort bears M. W. Heron's signature on the label.

Samuel Adams Beer

St. Louis is home to many beers, but it's a little known fact that Sam Adams is one of them. Samuel Adams beer was started by Jim Koch, who got his JD and MBA from Harvard. But when it came to getting a beer recipe, well, he got that from St. Louis.

Jim's great-great grandfather Louis Koch started brewing Louis Koch Lager in Soulard in 1860. Louis's son Charles Jerome worked as a brewmaster around St. Louis, as did his son Charles Joseph, who actually invented an important malt process.

Guess what his son Charles Joseph Koch Jr. did for a living? He was a brewmaster.

By the time baby boomer Jim Koch finished all that Harvard education, he took the recipe for Louis Koch Lager, made some test batches, and changed the name to Samuel Adams Boston Lager.

Why Boston? That's where Jim was living, and that's where he began walking from pub to pub asking bartenders to sell his product.

Koch launched Samuel Adams in April 1985. Six weeks later, it was named Best Beer in America.

Of course it won—it was a St. Louis recipe!

Kurt von Schuschnigg–The World Leader Who Moved to St. Louis After World War II

Kurt von Schuschnigg became chancellor of Austria in 1934 after ten Austrian Nazis assassinated Engelbert Dollfuss. Von Schuschnigg attempted to keep friendly relations with the Third Reich. In fact, he went so far as to define Austria as a German state. While personally rejecting National Socialism, von Schuschnigg freed thousands of Nazis from Austrian prisons as a way to achieve recognition and independence from Hitler.

But things started to fall apart for Austria when Mussolini argued against its independence in 1937.

When Hitler insisted von Schuschnigg appoint a Nazi as interior minister in control of the police, von Schuschnigg resisted. Instead, he called for elections to determine if the Austrian people wanted a "free and German, independent and social, Christian and united" country.

Hitler was furious and annexed Austria in 1938. During the *Anschluss*, von Schuschnigg was kept under Gestapo surveillance and then sent to Dachau and various other concentration camps until the end of World War II.

After the war, Kurt von Schuschnigg became a professor at Saint Louis University in 1947 and an American citizen in 1956.

Marshall McLuhan (The Medium Is the Message) Taught at SLU

"You know nothing of my work. How you got to teach a course in anything is amazing."

Those words were spoken by Marshall McLuhan in Woody Allen's 1977 movie *Annie Hall*. St. Louisans may know of his work, but few know the Canadian philosopher of communication theory taught at Saint Louis University for six years. In fact, McLuhan's stint at SLU is not even included in *Better the Dream*, a history of the school published in 1968.

McLuhan taught in the school's English Department starting in 1938. He left in 1944, shortly after being classified 1A by the St. Louis Draft Board, to head up the English Department at Assumption College in Windsor, Ontario.

Later, he coined the phrases "global village" and "the medium is the message." As a communications theorist, McLuhan sought to explain how electronic media affected people, oftentimes in ways they did not know.

McLuhan loved intellectual discourse in St. Louis with debates over pasta dinners at faculty homes. He would pass out Shakespearean plays at parties and assign roles to attendees. One night McLuhan was arguing in a St. Louis saloon with an open copy of James Joyce's *Finnegan's Wake* on the bar. A patron stumbled upon it, read a page, and then said, "My God, I really am drunk."

Section Seven

Dark St. Louis

Dr. Joseph Nash McDowell

Dr. Joseph Nash McDowell is a character in the Seth Grahame-Smith novel and movie *Abraham Lincoln: Vampire Hunter*. Grahame-Smith depicts McDowell as the proprietor of a vampire blood bank who later starts a medical college fortified by armaments.

The account is not entirely fictional. McDowell started Missouri Medical College on Gratiot Street in St. Louis in 1840, but he was not your run-of-the-mill medical school dean, at least by twenty-first-century standards.

In 1848, McDowell was accused of abducting a woman for body parts, and his facility was almost stormed by alarmed, stone-throwing protestors. Historian Charles van Ravenswaay states McDowell held his ground with a stockpile of 1,400 muskets and three cannons stored behind his school's six-foot-thick walls. No shots were fired—the crowd dispersed when the doctor aimed a cannon in its direction. The woman turned up safe in Alton, Illinois.

I'm not sure how many medical schools currently have their own artillery. But wait, the story gets better.

On another occasion, when McDowell was accused of grave-robbing, he fended off the angry mob with a bear he kept on the school grounds. That's right, a bear. When they said it was tough getting into that medical school, they weren't kidding!

McDowell wore a breastplate because he feared for his safety. However bizarre, his wardrobe was probably prudent for McDowell was known to speak out against Catholics and immigrants. And if St. Louis had anything in the mid-1800s, it was Catholics and immigrants.

McDowell didn't likely win many friends by supposedly aiming his college's cannons at Christian Brothers College across the street.

McDowell's school had an inner column where he wanted to preserve his family's dead bodies in huge copper cylinders filled with alcohol. After McDowell's fourteen-year-old daughter Anna died of pneumonia, he preserved her body inside an alcohol-filled container in a cave in Hannibal, Missouri. To this day, the cave's tour guides relate the McDowell story.

During the Civil War, Major General Henry H. Halleck, commander of the Union Army's Department of the West, converted McDowell's medical college into a prison for Confederate soldiers and sympathizers. It became known as the Gratiot Street Prison.

McDowell died in 1868, but his medical school merged with the St. Louis Medical College to become Washington University School of Medicine in 1899. Today, Washington University is nothing like Dr. McDowell's nineteenth-century Missouri Medical College. Except for the school mascot— a bear!

Gratiot Street Prison

The Exorcist

While the movie *The Exorcist* takes place on the campus of Georgetown University, the "real life" exorcism upon which the book and movie are based has another Jesuit connection: Saint Louis University.

St. Louis's exorcism involved a boy in Maryland, identified by numerous websites as Ron Hunkeler, who was introduced to a Ouija board by his aunt from St. Louis. Soon, the boy's bed shook mysteriously, bibles flew through the air, and words like "Louis" appeared on his torso. The family decided to travel to St. Louis to visit family.

They stayed with relatives on Roanoke Drive in Bel-Nor. Things did not improve for the boy in St. Louis—he experienced pain and scratches on his body. His bed continued to shake for no reason. Father Raymond Bishop, a professor at Saint Louis University, poured holy water on the bed. It calmed things down temporarily.

Father Bishop returned with Father William Bowdern, pastor of St. Francis Xavier College Church. A bottle of holy water leapt across the room. Furniture rearranged itself. Father Bishop kept notes in a diary. As reported by Chad Garrison for the *Riverfront Times*, the unedited copy of Bishop's diary gave numerous details about the St. Louis exorcism.

The priests received approval from Archbishop Joseph Ritter to perform an exorcism on March 16, 1949. At this time, more markings appeared on the boy's body such as "Our Lord . . . His Blessed Mother . . . St. Michael," along with a picture of the Devil and the word "hell."

Fathers Walter Halloran and William Van Roo assisted

Bishop and Bowdern. The nightly exorcisms continued with the boy spitting in the priests' faces, wrestling them with great strength, punching and breaking Halloran's nose, speaking in a high-pitched diabolical voice, and writhing when sprinkled with holy water. On March 20, according to the diary allegedly kept by Father Bishop, the boy yelled, "Go to hell you dirty sons of bitches."

The priests moved the boy to Alexian Brothers Hospital on Broadway and Keokuk Street and then to the College Church rectory on the campus of Saint Louis University.

Questions Remain

With all the shouting and problems in Bel-Nor, why didn't any neighbors notice?

The attending priests remained quiet throughout the years until their deaths. Why didn't they chronicle and share their experience for the betterment of mankind? After all, they were educators.

Why hasn't any member of the media tracked down and interviewed Ron Hunkeler?

Why didn't the priests call in other medical professionals? Why wasn't the boy taken to another hospital—such as the Barnes Hospital Psychiatric Ward—for a second opinion and perhaps medication?

Why didn't the priests document the marks on the boy's body with a camera?

Perhaps we will never know the "real" story of the St. Louis exorcism.

On April 18, 1949, according to an account of the priest's diary as reported in the *Riverfront Times*, the boy was handed a crucifix at the hospital. He shouted back, "He has to say one more word, one little word, I mean one BIG word. He'll never say it. He has to make 9 Communions. I may not have much power always, but I am in him. He will never say that word. I am always in him."

At 10:45 p.m., all was still. The boy then released these words, "Satan! Satan! I am St. Michael, and I command you Satan, and the other evil spirits to leave the body in the name of Dominus, immediately. Now! NOW! N-O-W!"

The boy woke up and said, "He's gone."

Father Bishop's diary recounts the boy had a vision on that final day of a battle between the devil, his cohorts, and St. Michael the Archangel. St. Michael allegedly smiled and said to the boy, "*Dominus*"—Latin for Lord.

William Peter Blatty's novel *The Exorcist* spent fifty-seven weeks on the *New York Times* bestseller list and was in the number one position for seventeen weeks. The movie by the same name was a box office sensation in 1973.

An Author Who Wrote from the Grave

Patience Worth, one of the most successful authors out of St. Louis about 100 years ago, was never seen in St. Louis. Even though she entertained at parlor gatherings, answered her audience's questions, received praise by the *New York Times*, and became one of the top poets in 1917, nobody ever saw her face or heard her voice.

That's because Patience Worth supposedly died in the 1600s, and her seven books—as well as her volumes of poetry, plays, and short stories produced between 1913 to 1937—were channeled to the world via a Ouija board used by Pearl Curran, a St. Louis housewife with limited education.

Worth explained, through Curran, how she migrated to the United States in the 1600s, lived on Nantucket Island, and was killed by an Indian. In an old-fashioned English dialect, she spoke of culture, food, dress, architecture, and habits to which Curran, a former department store clerk, would seemingly have no connection.

How big a deal was Patience Worth?

Crowds gathered as Curran recited Worth's words. Curran's husband took dictation.

The *New York Times* hailed her first novel as a "feat of literary composition." The Joint Committee of Literary Arts of New York named Worth—or was it Curran?—one of the best authors of 1918. Biographer Daniel B. Shea points out, "Two of her poems in 1916 and five more in 1918 were reprinted in

William Stanley Braithwaite's *Anthology of Magazine Verse and Year Book of American Poetry*."

According to *Smithsonian Magazine*, Worth was "nothing short of a national phenomenon in the early years of the 20th century."

Various experts tried to explain Curran. Some said she had a multiple personality disorder. Others, skeptical at first, claimed an outside source seemed to work through her.

Was Pearl Curran a fraud? Possibly, but that was never proven.

According to Shea, Patience Worth occasionally used anachronistic words such as "lollipop." And she referenced ideas published in the late nineteenth century and available to the public, including Curran. But how was a St. Louis housewife able to produce 4 million words from 1913 until 1937, some of which attained critical acclaim? How did she quickly recite numerous poems and essays in front of parlor crowds?

Curran died in 1937 leaving behind one of the great literary mysteries of the twentieth century.

The Blues Player Who Hired a Hit Man

Hockey is a violent sport, but St. Louis Blues player Mike Danton took roughness to a new level in 2004. He was arrested and convicted for trying to hire a hit man to kill his agent and former coach David Frost.

The plan: Danton was to pay a hit man $10,000 to kill Frost and make the crime look like a botched burglary. Danton used a nineteen-year-old nursing student to locate the contract killer, who turned out to be a police dispatcher working with the authorities.

While many speculate Frost was overbearing and abusive to Danton, others suggest he and Danton had a homosexual relationship. Some insist Danton was paranoid due to drug misuse or abuse. Or, were Danton's estranged parents—whose surname was Jefferson—abusive and Danton's real targets? U.S. District Court Judge William Stiehl was perplexed. "I do not believe in over eighteen years on the bench I have been faced with a case as bizarre as this one," he said. Danton pleaded guilty to conspiracy to commit murder and was sentenced to seven and a half years in prison.

He served five years and returned to play hockey in Canada and Europe.

Jack the Ripper

Did Jack the Ripper, London's infamous serial killer, live in St. Louis?

Some speculate Dr. Francis Tumblety, a quack surgeon who lived on and off in St. Louis in the nineteenth century, may be responsible for the murders of prostitutes in London's Whitechapel district in 1888.

The Guardian newspaper described Tumblety as an "American quack doctor who was in London at the time of the murders. Named as a suspect in 1913 by former special branch chief JG Littlechild, Tumblety was a sadist and homosexual who kept female body parts in a cabinet in his home."

Tumblety sold fake Indian herb cures from his office above an oyster bar at 50 Olive Street between Third and Fourth streets in 1865. He lived at the Lindell Hotel on Washington Avenue between Seventh and Eighth streets. Tumblety was arrested on March 9, 1865, for impersonating a federal officer. He was also linked to the assassination of President Lincoln because he once employed David Herold, an accomplice of John Wilkes Booth.

What is the case against Tumblety?

Various accounts suggest Tumblety owned a morbid collection of women's internal body parts which he kept in glass jars. Jack the Ripper removed the internal organs of his victims. Also, Tumblety stayed in the unfashionable Whitechapel district at the time of the murders. He also was a misogynist who frequently scorned women, especially prostitutes.

Jack the Ripper left a note with the return address "From Hell." Tumblety once sent a letter from Philadelphia with the identical return address.

Tumblety was arrested in London after the Jack the Ripper murders and then released. He was later arrested in the same city for gross indecency, a charge often associated with homosexuality.

Tumblety disappeared from the scene for five years before returning in 1893 to St. Louis where he remained until he died in the city's St. John's Hospital in 1903. No direct evidence links Tumblety to the Whitechapel murders of 1888. *The Guardian* also notes about 140 individuals have been suspected of being Jack the Ripper.

Escape from St. Louis

Actor Donald Pleasence was known for portraying some rather brave people. In *The Great Escape*, Pleasence's visually impaired character Blythe, "The Forger," insists on making a daring escape from a German prisoner-of-war camp despite his handicap. Pleasence also gave us Dr. Sam Loomis, who chased the psychotic murderer Michael Myers through neighborhood streets in John Carpenter's *Halloween*.

However, when he got to St. Louis in the fall of 1980 to film John Carpenter's *Escape from New York*, Pleasence was afraid. He stayed at a hotel near the Arch and management warned him the downtown neighborhood wasn't safe. According to his costar Adrienne Barbeau, Pleasence took the warning very seriously. He hired a cab to take him to a restaurant directly across the street.

Before There Was Estee Lauder, There Was Arsenic

Throughout history, women pursuing beauty have employed oils, creams, lotions, and potions of all sorts. But St. Louis women in the nineteenth century probably used the most dubious of all cosmetic aids: arsenic.

Historian Kenneth H. Winn tells us mid-1800s women ate arsenic to acquire fair, white complexions. They got this idea from an 1851 report by Dr. T. von Tschudi which suggested Austrian peasants ingesting arsenic achieved improved looks and greater physical stamina. Before you go out and eat a bowl of arsenic, know that Tschudi also reported arsenic killed people. Somehow this aspect of his study was not translated or disseminated or both. In fact, arsenic, taken orally, leads to oxygen deprivation, organ failure, and cardiovascular collapse.

According to Winn, physicians and lecturers in the 1850s warned of arsenic's dangers and recommended its use be restricted to eliminating rats. Arsenic not only posed grave threats to women, they warned, but husbands could meet "untimely ends" if exposed to the exhalation of wives consuming arsenic. (And you thought your spouse had "bad" breath.)

On November 20, 1855, thirty-seven-year-old St. Louis wife and mother Kate Bennett died of arsenic poisoning. The poor woman, an arsenic user seeking a lovelier appearance, is memorialized to this day with a large grave monument at Bellefontaine Cemetery in St. Louis, founded in part in 1849 by her husband, William.

She was known as "the most beautiful woman in St. Louis."

Look Out for the Cheater

In 1966, Walter Scott, lead singer for the St. Louis rock and roll group Bob Kuban and the In-Men, sang the lyrics for "The Cheater":

Haven't you heard about the guy known as the cheater
he'll take your girl and then he'll lie and he'll mistreat her
it seems every day now
you hear people say now
Look out for the cheater
make way for the fool-hearted clown
look out for the cheater
he's gonna build you up just to let you down

"The Cheater," a smash hit for the group, peaked at No. 12 on the Billboard Top 40. But Scott could not possibly have known the irony of his lyrics.

In the 1980s, Scott's wife, Jo Ann, had an affair with home repair contractor James Howard Williams. Trouble followed. First, Williams' wife, Sharon, died in a violent car crash on October 19, 1983. Later, on December 27, 1983, Walter Scott disappeared. Although his car was found at Lambert Airport, he left no other trace.

On April 1, 1987, Sharon Williams' body was exhumed and examined. The medical examiner determined she had been struck in the head by another person and had not died in a car accident. She had been murdered.

James Williams' son, Jim Jr., was questioned by police. He told police to visit his father's home in St. Charles and look in a cistern disguised to look like a planter. On April 10, 1987, Walter Scott's body—hog-tied and wearing a blue and white jogging suit—was found in the cistern.

James Howard Williams, a true-life cheater, was found guilty of the murders of his wife, Sharon, and Walter Scott. On January 13, 1992, he was sentenced to life in prison without probation or parole. Scott's wife, another cheater, was found guilty of hindering the prosecution. She spent eighteen months in prison. Jim Williams died in prison in 2011.

Upon hearing of Williams' death, Walter Scott's mother, Kay, told the *St. Louis Post-Dispatch*, "I was wishing he would live longer so he would have to suffer a little longer."

"The Cheater," sung by Walter Scott, is still played on the radio. It is not the most popular song of our time but certainly the most prophetic.

Stay inside your door now
He'll hurt you once
Then turn around and
Hurt you some more now
Look out for the cheater

John Vincent: The Arch Jumper

Folks, don't allow your kids to read this entry. Go ahead, kid-dos, just move along. Proceed to the next story. There's nothing for you here.

OK then. We don't want anyone getting any crazy ideas. And for all those with eyes still on this page, you must promise *not* to imitate anything contained herein. In fact, it's best if you burn or eat this page after reading.*

Here goes:

The most daring and dangerous and asinine deed associated with the Gateway Arch took place on September 14, 1992. Before dawn, twenty-five-year-old John C. Vincent, a St. Louis native living in Harvey, Louisiana, climbed the monument using suction cups.

Even a small problem with the cups could have dropped Vincent to his death. And once he reached the Arch's apex, well, that's not exactly the lobby of the Ritz. It's a 630-foot drop unprotected by guardrails. So, the entire venture was extremely daring.

And what did Vincent do at the top? He jumped off with a rectangular "sport" parachute.

Vincent later told KSDK-TV he originally intended to climb and jump off Chicago's Willis Tower, then known as the Sears Tower. He scouted the Chicago sight, but security and logistics did not work out.

Vincent boarded a plane headed to his home in Louisiana with a stopover in St. Louis. Once here, he thought of scaling

---

*Unless you are borrowing this book from the library.

and parachuting from the Gateway Arch. He rented a car, drove downtown, and toured the Archgrounds. Not knowing when he would get another chance to visit St. Louis, he took in the movie in the Arch's underground museum.

Vincent proceeded to the St. Louis Galleria to buy a video camera and two-way radio equipment. He spotted a woman driving a car with the license plate "Danzig," a rock band. They struck up a conversation, hit it off, and she agreed to be his getaway driver. She recruited others to help as well. At her home that night, she introduced Vincent to two St. Louis men willing to record the stunt on videotape and drive a second getaway car.

Around 3 a.m. on the morning of September 14, 1992, John Vincent, using suction cups, climbed the north leg of the Gateway Arch in about two hours and fifteen minutes. Once atop, he said a prayer for Kenneth Swyers, the Overland, Missouri, man who tried a similar stunt on November 22, 1980.

Swyers, a Westinghouse employee and a veteran of 1,600 jumps, was supposed to jump from a plane, parachute to the Arch's top, and jump again using a second chute. But, with winds too strong, Swyers got entangled in his parachute atop the Arch and was blown down its north leg, falling to his death as his wife watched from below with a camera.

After the prayer, Vincent jumped off the Arch at 6 a.m. He glided to the ground in twenty seconds. He took off in the woman's getaway car, stopped at KSDK for an interview, and proceeded to Lambert where he boarded a flight to Louisiana.

However, all was not well. Vincent's male accomplices were arrested. Authorities were furious. Vincent was arrested and prosecuted. Three months later, John Vincent pleaded guilty to climbing a national monument and then jumping off of it, both misdemeanors. He gave up ownership of his photographs and videotape in exchange for a light sentence. He also agreed to testify against his male accomplices, Ronald K. Carroll and Robert H. Weinzetl.

He served three months at Federal Prison Camp Eglin in Fort Walton Beach, Florida, known at the time as a "Club Fed." He told Pat McGonigle of KSDK he "enjoyed the prison's tennis courts, beach volley ball, big screen TV, pool tables (and) really nice people there."

Vincent was last reported living in Hawaii.

It's now OK for impressionable minds to continue reading this book.

Courtesy JNPA

The Dueling Senator

Does it seem St. Louis is more violent today than during the "good ol' days?"

If so, consider the feud between St. Louis lawyers Charles Lucas and Thomas Hart Benton in 1816. The two disagreed over evidence in a court case and questioned each other's integrity. The simmering feud got hotter at a polling place when Lucas questioned whether Benton had paid his taxes and therefore had the right to vote. The thirty-five-year-old Benton then called the twenty-five-year-old Lucas an "insolent puppy." That was enough for Lucas to challenge Benton to a duel.

On the morning of August 12, 1817, Benton and Lucas met at Bloody Island, a small island on the Mississippi River just above St. Louis. The two men were accompanied only by their seconds—assistants who verified the duel's fairness—and their personal doctors.

At a distance of thirty feet, the two "gentlemen" fired at each other. Benton's knee was grazed, but Lucas got hit in the neck. A weakened Lucas declared himself satisfied but

Senator Thomas Hart Benton.
Courtesy Library of Congress

Benton wanted another exchange or the promise of another duel in the future.

After Lucas recovered, Benton sent him a challenge. The two met again on Bloody Island at 6 a.m. on September 27, 1817. At a distance of ten feet, shots fired.

Benton was not hit.

Lucas was struck in the heart and fell. Benton approached Lucas and expressed his regret. At first, Lucas was furious and declared Benton "murderous." Moments later, Lucas is said to have expressed forgiveness. Then he died, all because he couldn't stand being called "an insolent puppy."

Three years later, Thomas Hart Benton was elected to the U.S. Senate from Missouri.

Seriously. Do you think St. Louis is more violent today?

The Little-Known Lincoln Duel

In the summer of '42—make that 1842—a letter lampooning Illinois's state auditor James Shields appeared in the *Sangamo Journal* of Springfield, Illinois. Written by "Rebecca" from "The Lost Townships," it declared Shields "a fool as well as a liar," exaggerated his looks, satirized his abundant self-confidence, and made him very angry. In truth, Rebecca did not exist. Her harsh words were penned by thirty-three-year-old Abraham Lincoln, his then-friend Mary Todd, and her friend Julia Jayne. Lincoln, an attorney who represented the State Bank of Illinois before it went out of business earlier in the year, was unhappy when Shields decided Illinoisans could not pay their taxes with the bank's notes.

The incensed Shields knew the "Rebecca" letter was a fake and demanded the newspaper publicly identify its authors(s). To keep the women out of trouble, Lincoln permitted the newspaper's editor to reveal his name.

On September 17, Shields wrote Lincoln demanding an apology and a retraction. However, Lincoln, upset by some of the accusations in Shields's letter, refused.

Abraham Lincoln, 1858.
Courtesy Library of Congress

So Shields challenged Lincoln to a duel as a way to regain his honor. According to dueling code, the challenged party chose the weapons. Lincoln did not ask for firearms—perhaps because Shields was a military veteran and an expert shot. Instead, knowing his opponent stood at 5 feet 9 inches with short arms, Lincoln selected broadswords. At 6 feet 4 inches and with longer arms, Lincoln would have the advantage.

As dueling was prohibited in Illinois where offenders could receive five years in prison, Lincoln's duel was set for Missouri across the Mississippi River from Alton, Illinois, about twenty miles north of what is now downtown St. Louis.

On September 22, the two met to duel. Shared friends John J. Hardin and Dr. R. W. English stepped in and encouraged both to call it off. They convinced Shields to withdraw his "insulting" note. For his part, Lincoln would state he meant no disrespect to Shields's "personal or private character" and declare he conveyed words "solely for political effect."

Everyone shook hands, and Lincoln's dueling days ended.

According to historian David Herbert Donald, Lincoln learned to watch his words and refrain from insulting others. Lincoln never wrote another anonymous letter again.

Lincoln was humiliated for almost breaking the law and for letting his emotions get the better of himself. He and Mary Todd agreed never to discuss the incident again. Once, as president, a soldier questioned him about the near duel not far from St. Louis. Lincoln replied, "I do not deny it, but if you desire my friendship, you will never mention it again."

The incident did have a beneficial effect. Mary Todd was impressed that Lincoln took the fall for her involvement with the Shields matter. She renewed her engagement to Lincoln, and the two were married on November 4, 1842.

Saddam Hussein and TUMS

The antacid TUMS is made in downtown St. Louis and nowhere else. How far is its reach?

Former Army nurse Robert Ellis cared for Saddam Hussein following the invasion of Iraq by the United States and coalition forces in 2003. In his memoir *Caring for Victor: A U.S. Army Nurse and Saddam Hussein*, Ellis recounts how he once gave the detained Iraqi president a TUMS antacid tablet when he had a stomachache.

"He took the pills I gave him and turned them over in his hand thoughtfully. He said he had given them to his daughter when she had a stomachache. 'I break them in half for her,' he assured me."

Hey, wait a darn minute. I thought this book is supposed to be about St. Louis. What's this with Saddam in Iraq?

Well, Robert Ellis is a St. Louis native who grew up in the Pruitt-Igoe projects and still lives in the area. Every single TUMS tablet is manufactured in downtown St. Louis. The TUMS plant at Fourth and Spruce streets makes more than one billion tablets every year. Just goes to show you some St. Louis homegrown products are enjoyed all over the world, even by Middle East dictators!

The Ten Amazing and Often Overlooked St. Louis Sports Stories

When World Series Champs Moonlighted

In 1949, Yogi Berra from the Hill led the New York Yankees to a World Series championship over the Brooklyn Dodgers. He had led the Yankees in RBIs that year. Guess what he did in the off-season?

Golf in Palm Springs? Relax in Cabo? Work out in Florida?

No, that's what today's players would do. Even players on *last-place* teams.

After the World Series, the Yankee catcher and future Hall of Famer worked six nights a week as a greeter in Ruggeri's restaurant. The owner Henry Ruggeri put out signs saying,

> Your genial host Lawrence (Yogi) Berra, World Series Champion Yankee catcher, Greets You from Ruggeri's.

Berra later wrote, "Basically I greeted people during dinner hours. It wasn't the worst thing to do, and it paid some bills."

Not bad work, for sure, but this was the starting catcher of the New York Yankees, who had just won his second World Series ring in three years!

I have no clue what last fall's World Series champs did from November to January, but I know for sure it wasn't working in restaurants. Or anywhere else, for that matter.

How far players have come in the last sixty years!

Buck and Borghi–Together on Two Continents

How small is the world? You tell me after reading this story.

Before coming to St. Louis, the late, great KMOX sportscaster Jack Buck served in the army in World War II. He was assigned to K Company, 47th Regiment, 9th Infantry Division.

On March 15, 1945, shrapnel hit his left arm and leg in the town of Remagen, Germany. A medic arrived and bandaged Buck's wounds.

When Buck got to St. Louis in 1954, he recognized a goalie, Frank Borghi, at a soccer game. The two talked and realized they had both been with the 9th Infantry.

In 1975, Buck was emcee for a banquet honoring the U.S. World Cup team that upset England 1–0 in 1950. Borghi, the team's goalie, was seated next to Buck at the dinner. They discussed the 9th Infantry. Both, as it turned out, were also in the 47th Regiment. Even more coincidentally, Buck and Borghi discovered they were both in K Company.

So Buck wondered, how many medics served K Company after it crossed the bridge at Remagen?

Jack Buck

Only one, Borghi replied, because the other one was wounded.

Hence, Frank Borghi had to be the medic who tended to Buck's wounds in Remagen.

Small world, indeed! But the Remagen story has another amazing coincidence.

As Buck pointed out in his memoir, *That's a Winner,* he wasn't the only sports broadcaster wounded in Remagen. About the same time in 1945, Lindsay Nelson, the voice of the Mets, Giants, Notre Dame foot-

Frank Borghi

ball, and the Cotton Bowl, also served in the 9th Infantry and was wounded at Remagen in the left arm.

Buck and Nelson were both enshrined in the football and baseball halls of fame. Borghi is a member of the U.S. National Soccer Hall of Fame.

Jo Jo White's Amazing Offers

Jo Jo White grew up at 2 Rutger Street in South St. Louis. After attending Vashon and McKinley high schools, he received basketball scholarship offers from 250 colleges. White picked the University of Kansas and, from 1966 to 1969, was a two-time All-American scoring 1,286 points in four seasons.

He played in Kansas's now-legendary 1966 NCAA Tournament game against Texas Western. In the game, KU trailed 81–80 when White scored a basket with seconds to go in the second overtime. However, a referee ruled White's heel was out of bounds when he shot the ball.

Jo Jo White, at right, with Bob Pettit, in front, and the author in the KMOX studios

"Can you believe I still look at tape of that game? And my foot is not on the line!" White insists.

The game was featured in the 2006 movie *Glory Road*.

In 1968, White won a gold medal playing for the U.S. basketball team in the Mexico City Olympics.

Incredibly, White was drafted by the Boston Celtics of the NBA, the Dallas Chaparrals of the ABA, the Dallas Cowboys of the NFL, and the Cincinnati Reds of Major League Baseball.

He chose the Celtics and became a seven-time NBA all-star. He logged fifty-six minutes on the court in the famous June 4, 1976, triple-overtime playoff game against the Phoenix Suns— no players today average more than forty minutes per game.

White was MVP of that year's NBA Finals. Perhaps most remarkably, White did not miss a single game from the 1972–73 season through the 1976–77 season.

The Celtics have retired his No. 10 jersey and his Kansas No. 15 jersey hangs in the rafters of the Allen Fieldhouse in Lawrence, Kansas.

Full House for the World Series

During the 2006 World Series, the two managers—Tony La Russa of the Cardinals and Jim Leyland of the Tigers—were reportedly very close friends. That may be true, but it doesn't mean they were the closest of World Series managers.

The 1944 World Series pitted St. Louis against St. Louis, with the Browns of the American League facing the Cardinals of the National League.

To save money during the 1944 season, Cards manager Billy Southworth and Browns manager Luke Sewell actually shared an apartment in the Lindell Towers. During the season, it was not a problem because when one team was at home, the other

Billy Southworth

was on the road. When the Browns were out of town, Sewell's wife and daughters would head back to family in Akron, Ohio. When the Cardinals were on the road, Southworth's wife and kids would head back to the farm near Columbus, Ohio.

Sewell and Southworth even shared a closet.

However, what to do during the World Series when both teams would be playing at home?

Southworth reportedly told Sewell on October 1, before the Browns had won the pennant, "You go right ahead (and take the apartment). I have rooms available at a hotel and I'll just move in when we return home and I'll just proceed as if we were still out of town."

It also has been reported the Southworths managed to borrow another unit in the same building from a tenant who was out of town during the World Series. Which raises the next question: Who in his or her right mind would leave St. Louis when both the Browns and Cardinals were playing each other in the World Series?

Both managers drove home together from Sportsman's Park after the games. The Cardinals won the Series in six games.

The Greatest Baseball Promotion

What was the greatest baseball promotion of all time? Nickel beer night? Disco night? Pennant day?

Forget about it!

The hands down, without-a-doubt greatest stunt in the history of baseball took place in St. Louis on August 19, 1951, when the St. Louis Browns sent 3-foot 7-inch Eddie Gaedel to the plate to bat against the Detroit Tigers.

Browns owner Bill Veeck originally got the idea from New York Giants manager John McGraw, a friend of the Veeck family, who had talked about sending a midget to bat but never did.

Veeck, previously owner of the Cleveland Indians, acquired the services of Gaedel through a booking agent in Cleveland. He signed Gaedel to a contract and paid him $100.

Gaedel wore the uniform of the Browns' nine-year-old batboy Bill DeWitt II, whose father owned the Browns before Veeck. DeWitt's No. 6 was removed from the jersey and replaced with 1/8, as Gaedel was listed in the day's scorecard.

Gaedel's appearance took place during the second game of a doubleheader. Veeck billed the day as a special tribute to the fiftieth anniversary of the American League. All 18,000 fans

Gaedel's uniform is now on loan to the Hall of Fame in Cooperstown, New York, by its owner, Bill DeWitt II, current owner of the St. Louis Cardinals.

received cake, ice cream, and, with a small hint of things to come, a *small* can of Falstaff beer.

Between games, the crowd was entertained with a lineup that would have made Federico Fellini proud: Max Patkin, the "clown prince of baseball," performed at first base, an acrobat jumped on a trampoline at second base, and a musical quartet featuring baseball great Satchel Paige played at third base.

A giant birthday cake was wheeled into the stadium. Gaedel, clad in his Browns uniform, popped out. Yes, they actually played some baseball that day.

When Gaedel walked to the plate to bat for Frank Saucier in the first inning, Detroit manager Red Rolfe objected. When umpire Ed Hurley was shown Gaedel's contract, he ordered, "Batter up!" With a 1.5-inch strike zone, Gaedel walked on four straight pitches from Detroit pitcher Bob Cain. Reaching first base, Gaedel was immediately replaced by pinch-runner Jim Delsing.

Gaedel proceeded to the press box, where he answered reporters' questions and then retired from baseball.

Ten years later, Gaedel got mugged in Chicago. He managed to get back to his mom's apartment, went to bed, and died in his sleep. One person from baseball attended his funeral: Detroit pitcher Bob Cain.

Pennant Race Romance and Leo Durocher's Furniture

In 1934, the St. Louis Cardinals and the New York Giants were in a tight race for the National League pennant. That's usually a time when players focus, block out everything else, and "get in the zone."

Cardinals shortstop Leo Durocher had other plans. It was the last week of the season, and on September 26, with the Cardinals one game behind the Giants in the standings, Durocher did what no other player in that situation has ever *thought* of doing.

Leo Durocher

He got married.

With outfielder Ernie Orsatti as his best man, Durocher exchanged vows with clothing designer Grace Dozier in a judge's chambers in the Municipal Courts Building in downtown St. Louis.

Why didn't Durocher wait a week or so until the season ended?

Did he have to get married during the most exciting pennant race in National League history?

Cards player-manager Frankie Frisch wondered as much after the Cardinals lost later that day. "Can you imagine picking a time like this for the wedding?" asked Frisch.

But the Cardinals won the next four games, the pennant, and the World Series.

Durocher and Dozier divorced nine years later. However, their dining room set was later donated to the Archdiocese of St. Louis. It was procured by Monsignor Edward J. Sudekum from the St. Hedwig church rectory before it closed in South St. Louis.

Today, the set—a remnant of the strange pennant race romance—can be found at the Our Lady of Lourdes rectory in University City.

An NBA Final Fight–But not Between Players

Game 3 of the 1957 NBA finals took place at the old Kiel Auditorium. The game pitted the St. Louis Hawks against the Boston Celtics. The rivalry was so intense a fight broke out between the teams—but not among the players.

During layups prior to the game, Bob Cousy of the Celtics told his coach, Red Auerbach, he thought the basket was not at the regulation ten-foot height. Auerbach took out a tape measure to check.

Hawks owner Ben Kerner, at right, looks on as star player Bob Pettit signs his contract.

Hawks owner Ben Kerner took Auerbach's action personally, as if his integrity was being questioned. And maybe it was.

Kerner came running onto the court to give Auerbach an earful of expletives. Auerbach later recalled, "He called me a bunch of names and I just didn't want to hear him anymore."

The Celtics' coach threw a punch, which landed squarely on Kerner's jaw and sent him tumbling at mid-court in front of a capacity crowd.

Yes, you read that right: a coach punched the other team's owner.

"The next thing you know, Kerner and Red were rolling on the floor," Hawks great Bob Pettit later remembered.

The skirmish ended before game time. Auerbach walked away and Kerner, putting a handkerchief to his bloody nose, proceeded to his seats in the stands.

The *St. Louis Globe-Democrat* ran a headline the next day, "Auerbach vs. Kerner in Non-Title Bout." Sportswriter Joe Pollack described it as a "one-punch, no decision in which Kerner claimed victory."

As it turns out, the rim was exactly ten feet above the ground, the Hawks won the game, and the Celtics won the series. Auerbach was fined $300 by the league.

Years later, Kerner declared, "I love Red. He was great for the game. He may have punched me but I had a night for him in St. Louis the year he quit coaching."

Bill White:
A Commitment Is a Commitment

In the middle of September 1964, when the St. Louis Cardinals were six games out of first place and not considered playoff contenders, the team's first baseman, Bill White, agreed to be the featured speaker at the Webster Groves Christian Church on the upcoming October 15.

What ended up happening on the afternoon of October 15, 1964? The Cardinals defeated the New York Yankees in the seventh game of the World Series.

The Cardinals were World Champions!

So, considering the change in circumstances, White cancelled his appearance in Webster Groves and issued the church a rain check, right?

No.

Bill White, after his team won the World Series, showered, put on a suit, and drove to the Webster Groves Christian Church to serve as banquet speaker. "A commitment is a commitment," he later wrote.

It's no wonder this remarkable man went on to a successful post-baseball career as a longtime broadcaster for the New York Yankees and then president of the National League.

happenSTANce

Stan Musial, in a twenty-two-year career, had 3,630 hits which were evenly divided, 1,815 on the road and 1,815 at home.

Denny McLain's Game Prep

Let's say you're scheduled to be the starting pitcher in Game 1 of the World Series. To up the pressure, the opposing team is starting with the best pitcher in baseball. How do you prepare the night before the big game?

That was the question in 1968 for Denny McLain of the Detroit Tigers as he was about to square off against Bob Gibson of the St. Louis Cardinals.

The answer? McLain spent the evening before the game drinking, playing the piano, and "whooping it up" until 3 a.m. in the bar at the Chase Hotel.

According to McLain, ". . . (after) some of the others went to bed, Jim Northrup, Norm Cash, Don Wert, Joe Sparma, and our wives stayed there until the joint closed. This was the World Series, not a wake and we didn't know if we would ever have the opportunity to do this again."

That *might* have been okay if the game the following day was at night. But no, it was a day game. The next day, McLain recalled, ". . . I was tired from entertaining the entire joint right up until closing. We had a great time the night before the biggest game of our lives, dumb bastards that we were."

McLain gave up three runs and lasted five innings. St. Louis won 8–1 as Gibson struck out seventeen Tigers, a World Series record to this day.

Wimbledon 1975: St. Louis Versus St. Louis

Two of the greatest tennis players of the 1970s were from St. Louis. And reminiscent of the 1944 Streetcar World Series, it was St. Louis versus St. Louis for the 1975 Wimbledon championship.

Arthur Ashe moved to Richmond Heights in 1960 to attend Sumner High School. Two months after arriving here, he

Arthur Ashe outside his alma mater, Sumner High School

became the first African-American to win the National Junior Indoor tennis title. In 1968, he became the first black man to win the U.S. Open. He was also the first African-American to be selected to the U.S. Davis Cup team.

Jimmy Connors grew up in East St. Louis and Belleville, Illinois. Like Ashe, Connors practiced at the 138th Infantry Armory on Market Street. Connors won a record 109 men's singles titles from 1972 to 1989. Ranked the world's number one tennis player for five straight years, Connors won ten grand slams.

Wimbledon is the world's most prestigious tennis tournament. On July 5, 1975, the men's finals could have been called "The Battle of St. Louis." It was Ashe versus Connors.

The two battled beyond the tennis court. A few days before Wimbledon got under way, Connors filed a lawsuit seeking $5 million in damages after Ashe referred to Connors as "unpatriotic" for not playing Davis Cup tennis.

Ashe defeated Connors in a stunning upset 6-1, 6-1, 5-7, 6-4. He became the first black male to win Wimbledon.

Connors took the loss "pretty hard" but felt "he deserved to revel in his moment. Arthur's game was flawless that day."

Connors later dropped the lawsuit.

Endnotes

America's First City

North America's first imposing Suzanne Winckler, "Prehistoric Metropolis in Illinois," *New York Times*, September 10, 1989.

One of the best-kept Nathan Seppa, *Washington Post*, March 12, 1997, H01.

The city was larger than London at the time Ed Schafer, "Nation's Biggest Prehistoric Site to Get Face Lift: Illinois Seeking to Reclaim Much of Ancient Indian Cahokia Mounds," *Los Angeles Times*, May 18, 1986.

Monk's Mound Bill Iseminger, author of *Cahokia Mounds: America's First City*, interview with author, April 30, 2010.

The First Mobile Phone

Henry Perkinson Tom Farley, "The Cell Phone Revolution: The Idea Is 60 Years Old, But It Took Decades to Make It Possible and More Decades to Make It Commonplace," *American Heritage of Invention and Technology* (Winter 2007): 9-10.

By 1948 ATT www.corp.att.com/attlabs/reputation/timeline/46mobile.html

80 pounds Farley, 10.

The First Gas Station

druggist, bicycle shop Michael K. Witzel, *The American Gas Station* (Osceola, Wisc.: MBI Publishing, 1992), 15.

About 250 cars Jeff Daniel, "FILL 'ER UP: On the 100th Anniversary of the Filling Station, St. Louis Can Take Pride in Its Pioneering Role in Refueling," *St. Louis Post-Dispatch*, August 3, 2005, E1.

Braille

was not pleasing to the eye Andrew Razeghi, *The Riddle: Where Ideas Come From and How to Have Better Ones* (San Francisco: Wiley, 2008), 84.

even love letters C. Michael Mellor, *Louis Braille: A Touch of Genius* (Boston: National Braille Press, 2006), 108.

The First Index Fund

choked back the tears Jeannette Cooperman, *St. Louis Magazine* (February 2009): 102.

My younger brother jerry Interview with author, January 2010.
Run-of-the-mill Ibid.
We kept that place spotless Ibid.
$200 Cooperman, 102.
Vanguard 500 Index Fund was founded vanguard.com/bogle_site/bogle_
bio.html

The First Director of Central Intelligence

Cloak and Dagger Group of Snoopers Tim Weiner, *Legacy of Ashes: The
History of the CIA* (New York: Doubleday, 2007), 14.
I want to go home Ibid., 15.
There is an urgent need Ibid., 15.
chairman of General American Life Insurance Company "R. Adm. Souers
Dies: Adviser to Truman," *St. Louis Post-Dispatch*, January 15, 1973, 3C.

The First Cocktail Party

Eric Felten, "St. Louis—Party Central," *Wall Street Journal*, October 6, 2007,
W4, citing *St. Paul Pioneer Press*, May 1917.
100 gallons Stephen E. Ambrose, *Undaunted Courage: Meriwether Lewis,
Thomas Jefferson, and the Opening of the American West* (New York: Simon
and Schuster, 1996), 133.

A Football First

Jim Morrison, "The Early History of Football's Forward Pass," Smithsonian.
com, December 28, 2010.
Manly Wiley Lee Umphlett, *Creating the Big Game: John W. Heisman and the
Invention of American Football* (Westport, Conn.: Greenwood Press, 1992),
87.
Scatter the mob Ibid., 88.
I took the team (St. Louis) to Lake Beulah Ibid., 91.

The First Reports of the Titanic

Mary Delach Leonard, "PD Reporter Was Aboard Rescue Ship," *St. Louis
Post-Dispatch*, December 14, 2003.
Tim O'Neil, "Vacationing Post-Dispatch Reporter Was First to Report
Survivors' Stories," *St. Louis Post-Dispatch*, March 31, 2012.
Francis Hurd Stadler, Titanic Collection, 1912-1996; www.mohistory.org/
files/archives_guides/StadlerCollection.pdf.
James Barron, "After Ship Sank, Fierce Fight to Get Story," *New York Times*,
April 9, 2012.

The First Kindergarten

Worked to develop Lawrence O. Christensen, et al., *Dictionary of Missouri Biography* (Columbia: University of Missouri Press, 1990), 87.

She had three assistants James Neal Primm, *Lion of the Valley: St. Louis, Missouri, 1764-1980, 3d ed* (St. Louis: Missouri Historical Society Press, 1998), 325.

Led the entire nation Christensen, et al., 86.

More than 400 cities Carol Ferring Shepley, *Tales from Bellefontaine Cemetery: Movers and Shakers, Scalawags and Suffragettes* (St. Louis: Missouri History Museum Press, 2008), 38.

The First Desktop Computer

First computer to sit on a desktop Carol Ferring Shepley, *Tales from Bellefontaine Cemetery: Movers and Shakers, Scalawags and Suffragettes* (St. Louis: Missouri History Museum, 2008), 234.

ten free acres of land Ibid.

"heavy metal" and "steely dan" Charlie Brennan, with Bridget Garwitz and Joe Lattal, *Here's Where: A Guide to Illustrious St. Louis* (St. Louis: Missouri Historical Society Press, 2006), 21.

"Wild boys" John Taylor of Duran, Duran, interview with author, October 24, 2012.

Unmarked grave Lorin Cuoco and William H. Gass, eds., *Literary St. Louis: A Guide* (St. Louis: Missouri Historical Society Press, 2000), 184.

The First German-American U.S. Senator

Bribed a prison guard Lawrence O. Christensen, et al., *Dictionary of Missouri Biography* (Columbia: University of Missouri Press, 1999), 677.

utilized for munition purposes George McCue, *Sculpture City, St. Louis* (New York: Hudson Hills Press, 1988), 78.

The First African-American U.S. Senator

Law was seldom enforced Robert A. Brady, *Black Americans in Congress, 1870 to 2007* (Washington, D.C.: U.S. Government Printing Office, 2008), 54.

I sedulously refrained Ibid.

Imprisoned in Missouri in 1854 Robert C. Byrd, *The Senate, 1789-1989: Vol. 1, a Chronological Series of Addresses on the History of the Senate* (Washington, D.C.: U.S. Government Printing Office, 1991), 529.

150 pupils Eric Sandweiss, ed., *St. Louis in the Century of Henry Shaw: A*

View Beyond the Garden Wall (Columbia: University of Missouri Press, 2003), 22.

The earliest known Sue Thomas, *A Second Home: Missouri's Early Schools* (Columbia: University of Missouri Press, 2006), 111.

The First Tweet

200 million active David Knowles, "Happy 7th Birthday, Twitter. Here Are 7 of Your Biggest Moments So Far," *New York Daily News*, March 20, 2013.

www.biography.com/people/jack-dorsey-578280?page=2

By inventing Twitter, Ellen McGirt , "05_Square: For Making Magic Out of the Mercantile," *Fast Company*, www.fastcompany.com/3017331/most-innovative-companies-2012/05square.

What's most meaningful Jack Dorsey, interview with the author, August 29, 2013.

David Jackson, "Michelle Obama's First Tweet," *USA Today*, October 21, 2011; content.usatoday.com/communities/theoval/post/2011/10/michelle-obamas-first-tweet/1#.UUEYIjfD4_c.

McDonnell

On July 21, 1946 David R. Wallin, "McDonnell Corp Young But a Leader in Space," *St. Louis-Post Dispatch*, February 16, 1964, Part 2: 3.

The F-4 established 16 speed www.boeing.com/boeing/history/mdc/phantomII.page

Mercury and Gemini

"capsule" Larry Merritt, archivist and historian for Boeing's St. Louis operations, interview with author, May 21, 2013.

The First Skyscraper

It might seem obvious Dan Protess and Geoffrey Baer, *10 Buildings That Changed America* (Chicago: Midway, 2013), 35.

A lot of tall buildings Ibid., 38.

This was a great St. Louis moment Charles Brennan and Ben Cannon, *Walking Historic Downtown St. Louis: 250 Incredible Years in Two Hours or Less* (St. Louis: Virginia Publishing Co., 2000), 16.

The thing about the Wainwright WTTW-Chicago, *10 Buildings That Changed America*, May 12, 2013.

Saarinen raised the Arch's height Charles Brennan and Ben Cannon, *Walking Historic Downtown St. Louis: 250 Incredible Years in Two Hours or Less* (St. Louis: Virginia Publishing Co., 2000), 12.

The World's Tallest Human

The Alton Museum of History and Art

www.altonweb.com/history/wadlow

www.greatriverroad.com/cities/alton/wadlow.htm

Wally Moon

Brian Cronin, "Sports Legends Revealed: Did Wally Moon Coin the Term 'Flake' to Describe an Eccentric Person?" *Los Angeles Times*, April 6, 2010, citing Maury Allen, *Bo: Pitching and Wooing* (New York: Dial Press, 1973).

Paul Dickson, *The Dickson Baseball Dictionary* (New York: W.W. Norton, 1989), 329.

Gordon Jenkins

I'm watching Cash one night Bruce Jenkins, *Goodbye: In Search of Gordon Jenkins* (Berkeley: Frog, 2005), 281.

At the time, I really Robert Hilburn, "Roots of Cash's Hit Tunes," *Los Angeles Times*, August 22, 2006.

Charles Lindbergh

the most audacious feat of the century Scott Berg, *Lindbergh* (New York: G.P. Putnam's and Sons, 1998), 143.

The first and finest Ibid., 157.

Five centuries have been required Ibid., 170.

My greatest asset lies Charles Lindbergh, *The Spirit of St. Louis* (New York: Scribner, 1953), 169.

Gert Cori

Sy Brody, *Jewish Heroes and Heroines in America* (Hollywood: Lifetime, 1996).

John H. Exton, *Crucible of Science: Story of the Cori Laboratory* (London: Oxford University Press, 2013).

John H. Exton, professor of molecular physiology and biophysics at the Vanderbilt University School of Medicine, and investigator at Howard Hughes Medical Institute, interview with author, May 9, 2013.

The American Chemical Society website, Carl and Gerty Cori and

Carbohydrate Metabolis, portal.acs.org/portal/acs/corg/content?_
nfpb=true&_pageLabel=PP_SUPERARTICLE&node_id=525&use_
sec=false&sec_url_var=region1&__uuid=84e5830f-af73-423a-b6a6-
62b50c436661.

Barkley Wedding

"Barkley-Hadley Wedding Draws Cheers of Crowd," *St. Louis Post-Dispatch*,
November 18, 1949, A1.

7Up

Third best-selling www.drpeppersnapplegroup.com/brands/7up/
six hundred bottlers in the United States Dorothy Brainerd, "Seven Up
Among World Leaders in Soft Drinks," *St. Louis Post-Dispatch*, February
16, 1964, 8X.
Dewar Andrew F. Smith, *Fast Food and Junk Food: An Encyclopedia of What
We Love to Eat, Vol. 2* (Santa Barbara: ABC-CLIO, 2012), 71.

Puffed Rice

According to Vaccaro Pamela J. Vaccaro, *Beyond the Ice Cream Cone: The
Whole Scoop on Food at the 1904 World's Fair* (St. Louis: Enid Press, 2004),
123.

John Colter

The first explorer Hiram M. Chittenden, *The American Fur Trade, Vol. 2*
(Stanford: Academic Reprints, 1953), 717.
without a doubt Eric Jay Dolin, *Fur, Fortune and Empire: The Epic History of
the Fur Trade in America* (New York: W.W. Norton, 2010), 182.
Fee Fee Baptist Charles G. Clarke, *The Men of the Lewis and Clark Expedition*
(Glendale, Calif.: A.H. Clark and Co., 1970), 47.

The First Interstate

The first project to go to construction U.S. Department of Transportation,
Federal Highway Administration, www.fhwa.dot.gov/interstate/faq.
htm#question10

Lyon

Sixty thousand Springfield James Neal Primm, *Lion of the Valley: St. Louis,
Missouri, 1764-1980, 3d ed* (St. Louis: Missouri Historical Society Press,
1998), 234-236.

Frost campus archon.slu.edu/?p=creators/creator&id=33: Frost Family
(1823-1960) | Saint Louis University Libraries Special Collections:
Archives and Manuscripts

A First U.S. Summer Olympics

purposeful dehydration "Past Imperfect: The 1904 Olympic Marathon
May Have Been the Strangest Ever," smithsonianmag.com, August 7,
2012.

ripped his stomach lining Ibid.

dodge cross-town traffic Ibid.

severely injured John Hanc, *The Coolest Race on Earth: Mud, Madmen,
Glaciers and Grannies of the Antarctic Marathon* (Chicago: Chicago Review
Press, 2009), 49.

if a dog hadn't chased him George R. Matthews, *America's First Olympics:
The St. Louis Games of 1904* (Columbia: University of Missouri Press,
2005), 137.

The First African-American Olympian(s)

Poage was the colored George Matthews, *America's First Olympics: The St.
Louis Games of 1904* (Columbia: University of Missouri Press, 2005),
146.

Chuck Berry

Fifty-five years ago Neill Strauss, "American Visionary," *Rolling Stone*
(September 2, 2010): 62.

It's very difficult for me Keith Richards, Rock and Roll Hall of Fame
Induction Ceremony, October 16, 1986.

If you tried to give rock and roll Taylor Hackford, director, *Chuck Berry
Hail! Hail! Rock 'n' Roll*, 1986.

I could never overstress Keith Richards, *Life* (New York: Little Brown,
2011).

If you want to learn rock and roll Phone call from Joe Perry to author's
voicemail, July 29, 2011.

Grant

defeated secession H. W. Brands, *The Man Who Saved the Union: Ulysses
Grant in War and Peace* (New York: Doubleday, 2012), 636.

was more secure Ibid.

Dred Scott

"The Dred Scott Decision," Old Courthouse Museum, National Park Service, U.S. Department of the Interior, Jefferson National Expansion Memorial.

Blackmun

using the club's fifth floor Dan Barks, interview with author, April 22, 2013.

I've been a Republican John McGuire, "Blackmun Shuns Tags on How He Rules," *St. Louis Post-Dispatch*, April 15, 1970.

He usually follows Ibid.

Strict constructionist James Millstone, "Blackmun Nomination to Court Predicted," *St. Louis Post-Dispatch*, April 14, 1970.

one of the Court's most liberal billmoyers.com/2013/01/25/moyers-moment-1987-justice-harry-blackmun-on-roe-v-wade/

William H. Webster

I talked to chief justice Interview with author, February 2010.

Wonderful Ibid.

I had scouting Ibid.

In nine years Philip Shenon, "The Reagan White House: Man in the News Webster of F.B.I. Named by Reagan as C.I.A. Director; A Reputation for Integrity: William H. Webster," *New York Times*, March 4, 1987.

I didn't invent the idea Interview with author, February 2010.

As a result Ibid.

French wine

destroyed 2½ million acres Allen J. Tobin and Jennie Dusheck, *Asking About Life 3rd ed* (Belmont: Thomson-Brooks/Cole: 2005), 627.

In 1870 Thomas Pinney, *A History of Wine in America: From Beginnings to Prohibition, Vol. 1* (Berkeley, University of California Press, 1989), 392.

He was awarded the C. Michael Smith, *Plant Resistance to Arthropods: Molecular and Conventional Approaches* (Dordrecht, Netherlands: Springer, 2005), 2.

Pieta

I am Jesus Christ Megan Friedman, "Michaelangelo's Pietà: Look, But Don't Touch," *Time*, January 26, 2010.

I leaped up and grabbed Anne-Marie O'Neill, "Creature Features: Bob Cassilly's Giant Animal Statues Encourage Little Kids to Think Big," *People* 48, no. 23, December 8, 1997.

landed at least one Frank Peters, "Honeymoon Highlight—Punch for Pietà," *St. Louis Post-Dispatch*, 1972.

Du Sable

The first white man Odie Hawkins, *Black Chicago: A History of America's Heartland, A History That Is Black* (Los Angeles: Holloway House, 1992), 11.

Second and Decatur streets Steve Ehlmann, *Crossroads: A History of St. Charles County, Missouri* (St. Charles, Mo.: Lindenwood University Press, 2004), 27.

Pontiac

Charles Brennan and Ben Cannon, "Chief Pontiac, the Native American Whose Actions Led to the American Revolution, Is Buried Here," *St. Louis Post-Dispatch*, July 3, 2000.

Earl Weaver

I was the first person to use it Earl Weaver, interview with author, July 12, 2009.

Baby Tooth Survey

The Committee for Nuclear Information. The group later became known as the Committee for Environmental Information.

325,000 baby teeth were collected "As Small as a Japanese Beetle," Washington University Archives, St. Louis Baby Tooth Survey (CEI).

50 times as much strontium-90 Dennis Hevesi, "Dr. Louise Reiss, Who Helped Ban Atomic Testing, Dies at 90," *New York Times*, January 10, 2011.

this treaty can be a step towards John F. Kennedy, Address to the Nation, July 26, 1963.

The treaty has halted Michael Egan, *Barry Commoner and the Science of Survival: The Remaking of American Environmentalism* (Cambridge: MIT Press, 2007), 75.

Mexican Revolution

Chaz Bufe and Mitchell Cowen Verter, ed., *Dreams of Freedom: A Ricardo Flores Magon Reader* (Oakland: AK Press, 2005), 36–42.

William Sherman

People may starve H. W. Brands, *The Man Who Saved the Union: Ulysses Grant in War and Peace* (New York: Doubleday, 2012), 323.

the roads which make Ibid.

at least a step in the direction Jay Tolson, "The Man Who Would Shape the Future of War: General Sherman's Destructive Path Blazed a New Strategy," *U.S. News and World Report* (July 2, 2007): 39.

opened the way to Ibid.

Jimmy Doolittle

the first genuine American hero Albin Krebs, "James Doolittle, 96, Pioneer Aviator Who Led First Raid on Japan, Dies," *New York Times*, September 28, 1993.

One man was killed bailing out over Ibid.

a factor that played an important role Ibid.

Israel

Mr. President Michael Beschloss, *Presidential Courage: Brave Leaders and How They Changed America, 1789-1989* (New York: Simon and Schuster, 2007), 197.

If you follow Ibid.

Someday...would have their own homeland Ibid., 221.

Never spoke to Clifford Ibid., 226.

Larry Conners' Sex Research

He makes that whore house Al Reinert, "Closing Down La Grange," *Texas Monthly* (October 1973): 52.

I took one of the girls Mark Babineck, "Chicken Ranch Memories Live on 30 Years After Bordello's Demise," *Associated Press*, July 19, 2003.

Inside work Reinert, 56.

Conners went undercover Gary Taylor, *I, the People: How Marvin Zindler Busted the Best Little Whore House in Texas* (Houston: Taylor, 2012), 35.

The Walker and Davis Cups

a player for Great Britain fell ill www.usga.org/WalkerCup/
ChampEventContent.aspx?id=21474853292

on the boards of seventeen corporations Kevin Phillips, *American
Dynasty: Aristocracy, Fortune, and the Politics of Deceit in the House of Bush*
(New York: Viking, 2004), 24.

the first public tennis courts Lawrence O. Christensen, et al., *Dictionary of
Missouri Biography* (Columbia: University of Missouri Press, 1999), 233.

Eads's Ironclads

entirely unsafe and impracticable Carl Charlson, "Secrets of a Master
Builder," *PBS American Experience*, October 30, 2000.

Eight boats were built Charles van Ravenswaay, *Saint Louis: An Informal
History of the City and Its People, 1764-1865* (St. Louis: Missouri Historical
Society Press, 1991), 501.

exceeded in terror anything Florence Dorsey, *Road to the Sea: The Story of
James B. Eads and the Mississippi River* (Upwey, Australia: Firebird Press,
1999), 67.

Eads Bridge

I think General Howard S. Miller, *The Eads Bridge* (St. Louis: Missouri
Historical Society Press, 1999), 120.

The Corps of Engineers Ibid.

Toussaint L'Ouverture

surprised Americans James Neal Primm, *Lion of the Valley: St. Louis,
Missouri, 1764-1980, 3d ed* (St. Louis: Missouri Historical Society Press,
1998), 69.

French Governor

William Barnaby Faherty, S.J., *St. Louis: A Concise History* (St. Louis:
Masonry Institute of St. Louis, 1999).

Charles van Ravenswaay, *Saint Louis: An Informal History of the City and Its
People, 1764-1865* (St. Louis: Missouri Historical Society Press, 1991).

James Neal Primm, *Lion of the Valley: St. Louis, Missouri, 1764-1980* (St.
Louis: Missouri Historical Society Press, 1998).

Three Flags

Charles Brennan and Ben Cannon, *Walking Historic Downtown St. Louis: 250 Incredible Years in Two Hours or Less* (St. Louis: Virginia Publishing Co., 2000), 23.

Cuba

Frederick A. Hodes, *Beyond the Frontier: A History of St. Louis to 1821* (Tucson, Ariz.: The Patrice Press, 2004), 121.

Mark Twain

I was incapacitated by fatigue through persistent retreating Charles Neider, ed., *The Autobiography of Mark Twain* (New York: HaperCollins, 1917), 134.

Jesuits Built SLU with Slaves

Priests' farm C. Walker Gollar, "St. Louis University Slaves," *Missouri Historical Review* 105, no. 3 (April 2011): 128.

slaves had to take care Ibid.

Napoleon Ibid., 129.

without exception good people Ibid.

humane and Christian masters Ibid., 127.

His poor parents Ibid., 133.

Violent and barbaric Ibid., 130.

Duschesne…owned slaves C. Walker Gollar, "St. Louis University Slaves," *Missouri Historical Review* 105, no. 3 (April 2011): 126.

Rosati appears to have prevailed Anthony J. Sestric, *57 Years: A History of the Freedom Suits in the Missouri Courts* (St. Louis: Reedy Press, 2012), 97-98.

The Grants Had Slaves

Confederate women H. W. Brands, *The Man Who Saved the Union: Ulysses Grant in War and Peace* (New York: Doubleday, 2012), 283.

Forest Park

no figure of a Confederate Caroline Loughlin and Catherine Anderson, *Forest Park* (St. Louis: The Junior League and University of Missouri Press, 1986), 133.

A pest George McCue, *Sculpture City, St. Louis* (New York: Hudson Hills Press, 1988), 77.

Suitable for a wedding cake Ibid.

Grotesque Ibid.

American Revolution

Eighty-five boatmen James Neal Primm, *Lion of the Valley: St. Louis, Missouri, 1764-1980, 3d ed* (St. Louis: Missouri Historical Society Press, 1998), 40.

POWs

Walked to a filling station David Fiedler, *The Enemy Among Us: POWs in Missouri During World War II* (St. Louis: Missouri Historical Society, 2003), 291.

Got their knuckles broken Ibid., 314.

South America Ibid., 303.

Drive trucks Ibid., 281.

Christmas cards Ibid., 304.

Roswell Field

I therefore write this Kenneth C. Kaufman, *Dred Scott's Advocate: A Biography of Roswell M. Field* (Columbia: University of Missouri Press, 1996), 60.

By the force Ibid., 68.

It was her wish Ibid., 69.

Lloyd Gaines

thirty-six African-American lawyers David Stout, "A Supreme Triumph, Then into the Shadows," *New York Times*, July 12, 2009.

Steppingstone toward Ibid.

Communist Auditor

George Lipsitz, *The Sidewalks of St. Louis—Places, People and Politics in an American City* (Columbia: University of Missouri, 1991), 97.

Republican National Convention

Is it not likely to be very warm in St. Louis? Harper Barnes, *Standing on a Volcano: The Life and Times of David Rowland Francis* (St. Louis: Missouri Historical Society Press, 2001), 91.

Wash U

Candace O'Connor, *Beginning A Great Work: Washington University in St. Louis, 1853-2003* (St. Paul: Litho, 2003), 6-8.

Auguste Chouteau

supervise the initial construction James Neal Primm, *Lion of the Valley: St. Louis, Missouri, 1764-1980, 3d ed* (St. Louis: Missouri Historical Society Press, 1998), 9.

Founding Date

sent young (Auguste) Chouteau Charles van Ravenswaay, *Saint Louis: An Informal History of the City and Its People, 1764-1865* (St. Louis: Missouri Historical Society Press, 1991), 18-20.

On February 14, 1764 James Neal Primm, *Lion of the Valley: St. Louis, Missouri, 1764-1980, 3d ed* (St. Louis: Missouri Historical Society Press, 1998), 7.

Oddly shaped J. Frederick Fausz, *Founding St. Louis: First City of the New West* (Charleston, S.C.: The History Press, 2011), 104.

We have many interesting Tim O'Neil, "Date of St. Louis' Founding Is Disputed," *St. Louis Post-Dispatch*, February 14, 2010.

even though it fell Fausz, 219.

Dream Team

"William Clark's Indian Museum: A Tradition Continued," National Park Service, Department of the Interior, October 1997: www.nps.gov/jeff/historyculture/upload/indian_museum.pdf.

General Bowen

U.S. Grant, *Personal Memoirs of U.S. Grant* (New York: De Vinne Press, 1885), 466-468.

H.W. Brands, *The Man Who Saved the Union: Ulysses Grant in War and Peace* (New York: Random House, 2012), 243-245.

Lee sent a note H. W. Brands, *The Man Who Saved the Union: Ulysses Grant in War and Peace* (New York: Doubleday, 2012), 365.

Pete, let's have another game of brag Shelby Foote, *The Civil War: Red River to Appomattox, 1st ed* (New York: Random House, 1974), 955.

served as Grant's best man! Charles Bracelen Flood, *Grant and Sherman: The Friendship That Won the Civil War* (New York: Farrar, Strauss and Giroux, 2005), 19.

Clark Clifford and William McChesney Martin Jr.

Boy wonder of wall street Melody Petersen, "William McChesney Martin, 91, Dies," *New York Times*, July 29, 1998.

Doubles partners John McGuire, "Soldan," *St. Louis Post-Dispatch*, March 19, 1982.

"St. Louis Blues"

Second only to silent night Joel Whitburn, *Joel Whitburn's Pop Memories, 1890-1954: The History of American Popular Music Compiled from America's Popular Music Charts, 1890-1954* (Ann Arbor, Mich.: Record Research, 1986), 192.

Joseph E. Johnston

David R. Kaufman, *Peachtree Creek: A Natural and Unnatural History of Atlanta's Watershed* (Athens: University of Georgia Press, 2007), 137.

If I were in his place… Alan Axelrod, *Generals South, Generals North: The Commanders of the Civil War Reconsidered* (Guilford, Conn.: Globe Pequot Press, 2011), 26.

Disney

It's great to see a city Dan Viets, "Mickey on the Mississippi: Walt Disney's Vision for Downtown St. Louis," *Gateway Heritage* 21, no. 1 (Summer 2000): 7.

would make parts of Disneyland obsolete Ibid., 8.

Rowdies Ibid., 9.

Any man who would build Ibid., 9-10.

Any plans developed by Mr. Disney Ibid., 10.

Can't Mr. Disney realize Ibid.

The U.N.

Edward R. Stettinius Steve Ehlmann, *Crossroads: A History of St. Charles County, Missouri* (St. Charles: Lindenwood University Press, 2004), 269.

And C. H. Spink Charlene Mires, *Capital to the World: The Race to Host the United Nations* (New York: New York University Press, 2013), 242.

Air Force Academy

fake beard, sunglasses and old clothes Diana Jean Schemo, *Skies to Conquer: A Year Inside the Air Force Academy* (Hoboken, N.J.: Wiley and Sons, 2010), 5.

I think I can fly R. I. Preston, et al., *Stetson, Pipe and Boots—Colorado's Cattleman Governor* (Bloomington, Ind.: Trafford, 2006), 287.

Symington personally favored Alton James C. Olson, *Stuart Symington: A Life* (Columbia: University of Missouri Press, 2003), 128.

Christian Scientists Principia website: itsatotallydifferentexperience.com/setting.htm

Elizabeth Keckley

Best living friend Diane Cole, "Dressing Up for History: A Seamstress Traveled from Slavery to the White House," *U.S. News and World Report* (July 2, 2007): 40.

Josephine Baker

biographer Bennetta Jules-Rosette Kaima L. Glover, "Postmodern Homegirl," *New York Times*, June 3, 2007.

Forty-thousand love letters David Wallechinsky and Irving Wallace, *The People's Almanac* (Garden City, N.J.: Doubleday, 1975), 899.

The thought comes Ibid.

Ted Kulongoski

At the orphanage Henry Willis, "Ted Kulongoski: A Political Player Who Really Enjoys the Game," *Eugene Register Guard*, April 8, 1979.

Bill Smith Bill Bishop, "Candidates Share Careers in Public Service," *Eugene Register Guard*, September 28, 1992.

Spinks Brothers

362 had no toilets Tim Fox, ed., *Where We Live: A Guide to St. Louis Communities* (St. Louis: Missouri Historical Society Press, 1995), 68.

too little space Ibid.

enough recreational space Ibid.

Attacking Ali's kidneys and left shoulder Bob Broeg, *The 100 Greatest Moments in St. Louis Sports* (St. Louis: Missouri Historical Society Press, 2000), 164.

Mackie Shillstone Ibid., 180.

Tennessee Williams

I got eliminated Lyle Leverich, *Tom: The Unknown Tennessee Williams* (New York: Crown, 1995), 211.

Never a more ignominious failure! Ibid., 215.

Brilliant and prolific www.pbs.org/wnet/americanmasters/episodes/ tennessee-williams/about-tennessee-williams/737/

one of the greatest playwrights in American history Ibid.

one of America's greatest artists performingarts.georgetown.edu/ tenncentfest/festival/

Joseph Conway

The blood ran down his back from the scalp wounds Walter Barlow Stevens, *St. Louis: The Fourth City, 1764 to 1909, Vol. 1* (St. Louis: S.J. Clarke Publishing Co., 1911), 289.

"Ripley's Believe It or Not" Joe Sonderman, *St. Louis People 365* (St. Louis: Stellar Press, 2003), 243.

Ulysses S. Grant

Poor and forlorn H.W. Brands, *The Man Who Saved the Union: Ulysses Grant in War and Peace* (New York: Doubleday, 2012), 78.

Crude and homely Ibid., 80.

I have worked hard Ibid., 85.

It is always usual Ibid.

I have seen many Ibid., 86

Openly despised Ibid., 94.

He sat humbly Ibid., 94.

The books were in confusion Ibid.
He was a sad man Ibid.
No terms Ibid., 165.
ungenerous and unchivalrous Ibid.

Caray and Hotchner

The other kids really gave it to me Harry Caray, with Bob Verdi, *Holy Cow* (New York: Villard Books, 1989), 17.
Hey, did you see that jacket A.E. Hotchner, *King of the Hill* (St. Louis: Missouri Historical Society Press, 2007), 201.

Cats

Missouri and the Mississippi have made a deeper Lee Ann Sandweiss, ed., *Seeking St. Louis: Voices from a River City, 1670 to 2000* (St. Louis: Missouri Historical Society Press, 2000), 556.
Yellow fog Jason Harding, *T.S. Eliot in Context* (Cambridge: Cambridge University Press: 2011), 14.

Francesca Simon

eighteenth bestselling author Brian MacArthur, "Bestselling Authors of the Decade," *The Telegraph*, December 22, 2009.

A Chorus Line

A downer Donna McKechnie, *Time Steps: My Musical Comedy Life* (New York: Simon and Schuster, 2006), 120.
You don't go to the theater Marsha Mason, interview with author, June 3, 2013.

David Merrick

not one of the nicest guys Burt Bacharach, interview with the author, May 9, 2013.
If you think this friggin' show Burt Bacharach, *Anyone Who Had a Heart: My Life and Music* (New York: Harper, 2013), 135.
We're missing a song Ibid.
the outstanding hit Ibid.

Colin Firth

Hideous Sandro Monetti, *Colin Firth: The Man Who Would Be King* (London: LBLA Digital, 2011).

Beethoven Calvin Wilson, "Classical Music a Highlight of Firth's Life in St. Louis," *St. Louis Post-Dispatch*, January 15, 2010.

Turned away at the door Dave Simons, interview with author, March 9, 2011.

Tom Cruise

I wanted to be an actor Peter Overton, "Cruise Control," *60 Minutes Australia*, June 5, 2005.

Mischievous Sue Lordi, interview with author, April 26, 2013.

Darth Vader

Bliss James Earl Jones, *James Earl Jones: Voices and Silences* (New York: Charles Scribner's Sons, 1993), 62.

Jean Lafitte

shove the Americans into the Atlantic Winston Groom, "Saving New Orleans," *Smithsonian Magazine*, August 2006, 59.

would forgive him for past smuggling Ibid.

the best Jackson received Ibid., 61.

Serenity Prayer

He's one of my favorite philosophers Laurie Goodstein, "Serenity Prayer Skeptic Now Credits Niebuhr," *New York Times*, November 28, 2009.

Oldest Recording of a Human Voice

John Schneiter, a trustee at the Museum of Innovation and Science, interview with author, October 25, 2012.

The Allman Brothers

the principal architects rockhall.com/inductees/the-allman-brothers-band/bio/

They had dancing girls Gregg Allman, interview with author, June 7, 2012.

Stormy Monday Gregg Allman, *My Cross to Bear* (New York: William Morrow, 2012), 76.

this little slice of town Ibid., 71.

were knocked out Ibid., 77.

Just wanted to get Ibid.

"Double Vision"

Davidson will be fine Lou Gramm, interview with author May 24, 2013.

St. Louis's Harbor

Russell Errett, interview with author, April 23, 2013.

Reddi-wip

750 employees John M. McGuire, "Made in St. Louis: We Were First in Shoes, First in Booze and Whipped Cream in a Can," *St. Louis Post-Dispatch*, November 21, 1999, C11.

He bought Cadillacs Nick Ravo, "Aaron S. Lapin, Reddi-wip Creator, Dies at 85," *New York Times*, July 14, 1999.

Peanut Butter

6 cents a pound Pamela J. Vaccaro, *Beyond the Ice Cream Cone: The Whole Scoop on Food at the 1904 World's Fair* (St. Louis: Enid Press, 2004), 115.

A sandwich a day keeps R.B. Fallstrom, "Peanut Butter Turns 100," *Los Angeles Times*, April 1, 1990.

peanut butter preparation process peanutbutterlovers.com/pb-lovers/pb101/history/

Kellogg's ground peanut butter Jon Krampner, *Creamy and Crunchy: An Informal History of Peanut Butter, the All-American Food* (New York: Columbia University Press, 2013), 35.

Original Manufacturers of Peanut Butter Ibid., 31.

O'Hare Airport

Larry Offner, "The Butch O'Hare Story," *St. Louis Magazine*, July 2005.

Michael Branigan, *A History of Chicago's O'Hare Airport* (Charleston, S.C.: The History Press, 2011), 52-62.

Wainwright Tomb

Charlie Brennan, "Charlie's Town," *Town and Style*, December 30, 2011.

Jacques Chirac

I've known the U.S. James Graff and Bruce Crumley, "France Is not a Pacifist Country," *Time*, February 16, 2003.

I still like a Bud Barbara Slavin, "Chirac Says He Has No Anti-American Feelings," *USA Today*, September 25, 2003.

Angels in America

Mormon contradiction Bruce Weber, "Angels' Angels," *New York Times*, April 25, 1993.

First idea for the play Sara C. Bixler, agent for Tony Kushner, interview with author May 21, 2013.

Halitosis

How about bad breath Gerard Lambert, *All Out of Step: A Personal Chronicle* (Garden City, N.J.: Doubleday, 1956), 97.

Always the bridesmaid Stephen Fox, *The Mirror Makers: A History of American Advertising and Its Creators* (New York: Morrow, 1984), 98.

Even your best friend Ibid., 97.

82 percent Lambert, 98.

$5 Million annually Fox, 98.

introduced Americans to halitosis History of Listerine, www.listerine.com.sg/history-of-listerine

Animal House

Never before have so few *The Hatchet*, 1966.

Ray Charles

Marci Soto, *Ray and Me* (St. Louis: Monograph Publishing, 2011).

Buzz Bissinger

Most powerful moments in life Angie Weidinger, "Maryville Talks Books: One on One with Buzz Bissinger," HEC-TV, 2012.

I will never forget it Imdb.

For the first time Buzz Bissinger, *Father's Day: A Journey into the Mind and Heart of My Extraordinary Son* (Boston: Houghton Mifflin, 2012), 132.

Southern Comfort

Cuffs and Buttons Sherre Day, "Southern Comfort's Creator Returns to Promote," *New York Times*, September 23, 2003.

M.W. Ibid.

Samuel Adams Beer

took the recipe Joseph H. Boyett and Jimmie T. Boyett, *The Guru Guide to Entrepreneurship: A Concise Guide to the Best Ideas from the World's Top Entrepreneurs* (New York: Wiley, 2001), 278.

Kurt von Schuschnigg

free and German Robert Wistrich, *Who Is Who in Nazi Germany* (New York: Routledge, 2002), 31.

Marshall McLuhan

My God, I really am drunk W. Terrence Gordon, *Marshall McLuhan: Escape into Understanding* (New York: Basic Books, 1997), 100.

Dr. Joseph Nash McDowell

McDowell kept attackers at bay Charles van Ravenswaay, *Saint Louis: An Informal History of the City and Its People, 1764-1865* (St. Louis: Missouri Historical Society Press: 1991), 342.

Preserve his family's remains Ibid., 521.

he fended off attackers with a bear Lisa Livingston-Martin, *Missouri's Wicked Route 66: Gangsters and Outlaws on the Mother Road* (Charleston, S.C.: The History Press, 2013), 24.

The Exorcist

Our Lord Chad Garrison, "Hell of a House," *Riverfront Times*, October 26, 2005, 24.

Go to hell Ibid.

He has to say Ibid.

Satan! Satan! I am St. Michael Ibid.

Linda Blair, interview with author, February 14, 2013.

An Author Who Wrote from the Grave

Feat of literary composition Gioia Diliberto, "Patience Worth: Author from the Great Beyond," *Smithsonian Magazine* (September 2010).

Two of her poems in 1916 Daniel B. Shea, *The Patience of Pearl: Spiritualism and Authorship in the Writings of Pearl Curran* (Columbia: University of Missouri Press, 2012), 1.

Nothing short of a national Diliberto.

lollipop Daniel Shea, interview with author, April 15, 2015.

The Blues Player Who Hired a Hit Man

I do not believe www.cbc.ca/sports/indepth/danton/

Jack the Ripper

American quack doctor Mark Honigsbaum, "Jack the Ripper 'May Have Killed Abroad': Murderer Possibly a Sailor Rather Than a Surgeon, Says New Book," *The Guardian*, May 2, 2005.

50 Olive Street Timothy B. Riordan, *Prince of Quacks: The Notorious Life of Dr. Francis Tumblety, Charlatan and Jack the Ripper Suspect* (Jefferson, N.C.: McFarland and Co., 2009), 104.

From hell Lisa Livingston-Martin, *Missouri's Wicked Route 66: Gangsters and Outlaws on the Mother Road* (Charleston, S.C.: The History Press, 2013), 16.

Escape from St. Louis

Adrienne Barbeau, *There Are Worse Things I Could Do* (New York: Carroll & Graf, 2006), 186.

Arsenic

Untimely ends Kenneth H. Winn, "Dying to Be Pretty: Arsenic Eaters in the Nineteenth Century," *Gateway* 29 (2009): 81.

the most beautiful woman in St. Louis Ibid., 75.

Look Out for the Cheater

I was wishing he would live Shane Anthony, "Man Who Murdered St. Louis Singer Dies in Prison," *St. Louis Post-Dispatch*, April 13, 2011.

John Vincent: The Arch Jumper

rectangular "sport" parachute Tim Bryant, "Man Pleads Guilty in Arch Jump," *St. Louis Post-Dispatch*, December 16, 1992.

Chicago's Willis Tower Pat McGonigle, "John Vincent Says He'd Jump Off Gateway Arch Again," KSDK-TV, February 25, 2013.

enjoyed the prison's tennis courts Ibid.

The Dueling Senator

James E. Moss, *Dueling in Missouri History: The Age of Dirk Drawing and Pistol Snapping* (Kansas City: The Kansas City Posse, 1966), 13.

The Little-Known Lincoln Duel

a fool as well as a liar David Herbert Donald, *Lincoln* (New York: Simon and Schuster, 1995), 91.

Insulting Ibid.

I do not deny it Ibid.

Saddam Hussein and TUMS

He took the pills Robert Ellis, with Marianna Riley, *Caring for Victor: A U.S. Army Nurse and Saddam Hussein* (St. Louis: Reedy Press, 2009), 81.

When World Series Champs Moonlighted

Yogi Berra, *Ten Rings: My Championship Seasons* (New York: William Morrow, 2003), 65.

Buck and Borghi

Jack Buck, with Rob Rains and Bob Broeg, *Jack Buck: That's a Winner* (New York: Sports Publishing, 2002).

Jo Jo White's Amazing Offers

Can you believe Jo Jo White, interview with author, May 9, 2013.

Jo Jo White, interview with author, June 6, 2006.

Full House for the World Series

Sewell's wife and daughters Richard Peterson, ed., *The St. Louis Baseball Reader* (Columbia: University of Missouri Press, 2006), 269.

You go right ahead David Alan Heller, *As Good as It Got: The 1944 St. Louis Browns* (Charleston, S.C.: Arcadia, 2003), 113.

Borrow another unit William B. Mead, *Baseball Goes to War* (Washington: Contemporary, 1998), 181.

The Greatest Baseball Promotion

Peter Golenbock, *The Spirit of St. Louis: A History of the St. Louis Cardinals and Browns* (New York: William Morrow, 2000).

Bob Broeg, *100 Greatest Moments in St. Louis Sports* (St. Louis: Missouri Historical Society Press, 2000).

Pennant Race Romance and Leo Durocher's Furniture

Can you imagine John Heidenry, *The Gashouse Gang: How Dizzy Dean, Leo Durocher, Pepper Martin, and Their Colorful Come-from-Behind Ball Club Won the World Series—and America's Heart—During the Great Depression* (New York: Public Affairs, 2007), 191.

An NBA Final Fight

Bob Cousy Hawks player Bob Pettit recalls Celtics player Bill Sharman complaining to Auerbach, but other sources attribute the complaint to Cousy. Bob Pettit, interview with author, May 9, 2013.

He called me a bunch Greg Marecek, *Full Court: The Untold Stories of the St. Louis Hawks* (St. Louis: Reedy Press, 2006), 57.

The next thing you know Pettit.

Auerbach vs. Kerner Marecek, *Full Court.*

I love Red Terry Pluto, *Tall Tales: The Glory Years of the NBA, in the Words of the Men Who Played* (New York: Simon and Schuster, 1992), 138.

Bill White

Bill White, *Uppity: My Life in Baseball* (New York: Grand Central Publishing, 2011), 95.

Denny McLain's Game Prep

some of the others Denny McLain, with Eli Zaret, *I Told You I Wasn't Perfect* (Chicago: Triumph, 2007), 116.

I was tired Ibid.

Wimbledon 1975

Pretty hard Jimmy Connors, *The Outsider: A Memoir* (New York: Harper, 2013), 161.

He deserved to revel Ibid., 157.

Index